Managing the Learning of History

Richard Brown

David Fulton Publishers
London

David Fulton Publishers Ltd
2 Barbon Close, London WC1N 3JX

First published in Great Britain by
David Fulton Publishers 1995

Note: The right of Richard Brown to be identified as the author of this work has been
asserted by him in accordance with the Copyright, Designs and Patents Act 1988.

Copyright © Richard Brown

British Library Cataloguing in Publication Data

A catalogue record for this book is available from the British Library

ISBN 1-85346-345-0

Typeset by Harrington & Co.
Printed in Great Britain by BPC Books & Journals, Exeter.

Contents

Foreword

The need for all teachers of history to achieve quality in their teaching and thereby ensure an effective learning experience for students is the theme at the heart of this book. It is Richard Brown's contention that quality will be achieved only when there is dialogue and collaboration between teacher and student, and between teachers working as members of a departmental team.

It is accepted that history teachers have been on the defensive since at least the early 1960s and that there has been only partial success in articulating a clear-cut case for including history in the secondary school curriculum, particularly at the post-fourteen stage. In the 1970s and 1980s, many secondary schools experimented with courses in integrated humanities. These were seen as posing a threat to the specific content and distinctive methodology of each of the subjects incorporated in the new conceptual framework.

To begin with at least, the arrival of the National Curriculum in 1988 appeared to enhance the status of history as a separate subject on the school timetable; but all this has changed with the recent Dearing Review which removed the obligation for all students to follow a history course at Key Stage 4. Once again, history teachers are having to fight for their place in the sun.

In this challenging and important book, Richard Brown makes clear that managing the learning of history is about developing a collaborative culture for the subject within a department, across the humanities and as an integral part of the whole-school curriculum.

Clyde Chitty
Birmingham
February 1995

QUALITY IN SECONDARY SCHOOLS AND COLLEGES SERIES

Series Editor, Clyde Chitty

This new series publishes on a wide range of topics related to successful education for the 11–19 age group. It reflects the growing interest in whole-school curriculum planning together with the effective teaching of individual subjects and themes. There will also be books devoted to management and administration, examinations and assessment, pastoral care strategies, relationships with parents and governors and the implications for schools of changes in teacher education.

Early titles include:

Active History in Key Stages 3 and 4
Alan Farmer and Peter Knight
1-85346-305-1

English and Ability
Edited by Andrew Goodwyn
1-85346-299-3

English as a Creative Art: Literary Concepts Linked to Creative Writing
Linden Peach and Angela Burton
1-85346-368-X

English and the OFSTED Experience
Bob Bibby and Barrie Wade
1-85346-357-4

Geography 11-16: Rekindling Good Practice
Bill Marsden
1-85346-296-9

Heeding Heads: Secondary Heads and Educational Commentators in Dialogue
Edited by David Hustler, Tim Brighouse and Jean Ruddock
1-85346-358-2

Learning to Teach – a guide for school-based initial and in-service training
Julian Stern
1-85346-371-X

The Literate Imagination: Renewing the Secondary English Curriculum
Bernard T. Harrison
1-85346-300-0

Moral Education through English 11-16
Ros McCulloch and Margaret Mathieson
1-85346-276-4

Partnership in Secondary Initial Teacher Education
Edited by Anne Williams
1-85346-361-2

Preface

All writers are, to some degree, parasitic. They begin by looking at the ideas of others and then modify them to suit their own thesis. This book is no exception. It trawls existing writings on management, industry and commerce as well as education, and uses them to make a case for changes in the way history departments in secondary schools are managed. My references show clearly my debt to these authors and to their experiences in managing far larger institutions than history departments.

I have taught in secondary schools for over twenty years and have learned much from my contacts and arguments with fellow teachers and students over that time. I am particular indebted to Dr. Hilary Cooper for her apposite critique of Chapter 2, to Barry Ellis, Curriculum Deputy at my school, for his valuable comments on content as well as style and to my department, especially J, Tom, Dave and Graham, for treating my ideas to vigorous reflection and criticism over the years. Without their healthy scepticism I would have found this book far more difficult to write. I have been particularly fortunate to teach for the past eight years in a school where my students have been unwilling to accept my ideas and methods without question. They have done far more than they realise in shaping my approach to teaching and learning. I hope that I have given them as much enjoyment as they have given me.

Above all I must thank Margaret for her support while I have been ensconced in my study researching, writing and revising the text. It takes a very special person to put up with someone who has written a book a year for the past fourteen years and who edits a national journal. This book is dedicated to her.

Richard Brown
December 1994

Introduction

In 1994 teachers faced the latest of nineteen Education Acts in fifteen years. These have caused a significant change in the way education is viewed and how schools are managed: what has been called a 'permanent revolution'. The 1992 White Paper, 'Choice and Diversity', claimed to establish an 'evolutionary framework' designed to complete the transformation of the education system of England and Wales begun in the 1980s. Just how 'evolutionary' the changes have been is a matter of some disagreement. For some, the changes begun with the Education Reform Act 1988 mark a decisive shift in education policy. There has been a move away from the post-war values of comprehensive provision in favour of earlier traditions of selective and private education. Ranson (1993) argues that this break marks a 'quiet revolution' in policy in which '"progression", "entitlement" and "local management" are substituted by a new [or renewed] emphasis on "specialisation", "selection", "autonomy" and "standards"'. Whatever the merits of this argument there is a 'quiet revolution' in management of schools from an approach that stressed the merits of quality development to one that focuses on the need for and development of quality learning.

The changes that have occurred in the last fifteen years have had a direct impact on the management of the learning of history in many ways, not least in the form of the National Curriculum. How far, however, has the management of history departments kept pace with the changes that have occurred? How far has managing become, for many teachers and heads of department, an administrative inconvenience or even irrelevance divorced from what really matters at the 'chalk face'? Are middle managers in history departments familiar with developments in management ideas and techniques? The development of alternative management structures and priorities in schools, a consequence in part of the developing National Curriculum, means that many of the older approaches to departmental management and the management of learning are now redundant, or at least questioned. The early experience of

OFSTED inspection and its published reports, with their references to inadequate departmental management, reinforce this viewpoint. Existing books on departmental management are, as a result, out-dated in their approaches and often fail to recognise sufficiently the symbiotic relationship between general curriculum and departmental management and the more specific management of learning. They are also general in scope, dealing with management issues either from a whole-school perspective or from a general departmental position.

The book takes as its theme the need for all teachers of history, and their heads of department or line-managers, to achieve quality in their teaching and in their students' learning. The issue is: how best can this quality be defined, achieved and maintained? Quality will only be effective and assured if there is dialogue and collaboration between student and teacher and between teachers within departmental teams. Underlying everything is the need for a reflective approach to teaching and learning in which there is a responsive attitude to the problem of student learning: how will the management strategy I've adopted help students to learn more effectively?

The first three chapters place the management of history teaching and learning in schools in its context. The opening chapter considers where history fits in the whole-school curriculum and what management problems this poses for teachers and heads of department. There will be some discussion of the debate on teaching history but the thrust of the chapter will be on the nature of, and contradictions posed by, a collaborative approach to teaching and learning within departmental, humanities and whole-school curricular settings. Chapter 2 asks: what is the nature of learning history and what management problems do teachers have to resolve? I am conscious that this is merely a sketch of a far more complex problem to which I hope to return later. The third chapter addresses the question of how quality learning and management can be promoted in history departments as part of the broader issue of improving standards in education. The remaining chapters deal with managing learning from a more practical perspective. Chapter 4 examines a collaborative approach to management. How can teachers contribute to a team approach to managing a history department and how can heads of department encourage such an approach? Chapter 5 considers how the process of Total Quality Management (TQM) can help history departments to clarify their goals and develop managing strategies that allow them to achieve continuous improvement in learning quality. Chapter 6 looks at evaluation and begins by asking: how can teachers evaluate student learning and evaluate departmental objectives? Then the appraisal of teacher performance is considered, through the twin processes of internal teacher appraisal and external inspection through OFSTED. Training teachers has become a central feature of government policy and Chapter 7 deals with the role of mentoring student teachers but extends this to consider teacher development within departments. The final chapter draws together the discussion of learning, teaching and effective team management.

The book is aimed at all teachers of history 11–18 who are concerned to manage student learning more effectively; at teachers of history who need guidance in planning to become a head of department; at those who are already heads of department and who need to refresh their management approaches; at those in initial teacher training who need a clear guide to being a history teacher and a member of a departmental team and, finally, at teachers acting as mentors within the new system of initial teacher training. All are encouraged to build on their existing good practice in a systematic way and to identify areas where radical change is needed. The book suggests solutions to the problem of managing learning history as we move towards the twenty-first century.

CHAPTER 1

History in the Whole-School Curriculum

'History matters. If we are to understand ourselves – our values, our institutions and our heritage, we have to understand our history. And by our history, I do mean *British* history...And knowledge precedes understanding. Children simply have to know the basic facts before they can start to analyse them and understand our historical development. To strip facts and chronology out of the study of history is as crazy as stripping grammar out of the teaching of English.'

Patten (1994)

The teaching of history and the content of the history curriculum in schools has been increasingly and overtly politicised during the last twenty years. There is nothing new in this. In countries like France, the United States and Japan there is a particularly strong emphasis in the curriculum on national history where, as Patten (1994) said 'To have national pride [is] seen as a virtue, not a vice.' In Britain, however, there is no clear consensus. The result has been twenty years of internecine trench-warfare between Right and Left, between traditionalists and progressives and between those who advocate content and those who see skills as the heart of the history curriculum. This chapter addresses these issues in the following way. First, we have to ask: where is history now? This will lead into a discussion of where history fits into the whole-school curriculum, and finally we shall consider the question of prioritising history and the management dilemma this creates.

Where is history now?

There is a 'great tradition' in the teaching of history that originated in the nineteenth century, the main features of which were fixed by 1900. The teacher was the dominant figure in this tradition, delivering the content of the past to largely passive students as a 'received subject'. The facts of British history were taught and tested. In this way the glory and story that was Britain was conveyed to generations of school pupils. This was challenged in the 1960s and the subsequent debate over the proper character of the history curriculum and how it should best be taught in school has been long and, in many respects, remarkably inconclusive. Mary Price's article 'History in Danger' is generally regarded as the clarion-call for the defence of school history against, in particular, the threat from humanities: 'There are not a few who are actually apprehensive about its future and see a real danger of history disappearing from the timetable as a subject in its own right.' Price (1968, p.342) and 'The tendency for half the population of secondary schools to drop the subject after three years seems to be increasing...does not indicate much security of tenure in the timetable or a very significant experience for the children.' Price (1968, p.343)

The process of appraisal had, however, begun earlier in the 1960s. The symposium *Crisis in the Humanities* (Plumb, 1964) had already examined the impact of the rapid extension of scientific and technical studies upon universities where previously the humanities had held a central and unchallenged dominance. The malaise facing history took on spiritual proportions: 'It has lost all faith in itself as a guide to the actions of men...and [its educational value] lies in the exercises it provides for the mind and not for what it contains.' Plumb (1964, p.9)

Plumb and Price raised issues that have dominated the subsequent discussions on history in the whole-school curriculum. What should the proper relationship between history and Society be at the end of the twentieth century? What should history in schools aim to achieve for all pupils? Price (1968) and Booth (1969, appendix iv, pp.145–8) both found evidence of increasing student frustration with history and that an Anglocentric emphasis limited the relevance of much content.

From 1969 to the mid-1970s all was change for history in secondary schools – or was it? The issue was one of curriculum reform through a critique of existing content and practice resulting in the emergence of the so-called 'new' history, so-called because, as Richard Aldrich has shown (Dickinson et al., 1984, pp.210–8), much of it was not new. An emphasis was to be placed on an 'evidential' and 'empathetic' approach – what was it like in the past and how do we know? – and upon history as a 'mode of enquiry'. Roy Wake, then HM Staff Inspector for History, wrote that 'We had also better accept once and for all that there are not historical facts; there is only evidence...' (Wake, 1970, p.153).

The 'skills-based' approach had its clearest exposition in the Coltham-Fines taxonomy of 1971, assuming that '...our decisions on...syllabuses ...should derive from our initial approach to historical thinking...Method, therefore, in its widest connotation comes first and knowledge takes second place.' (Ben Jones, 1973, p.26); it was also reflected in the establishment in March 1972 of the *Schools Council Project, History 13–16*. David Sylvester (1994, p.16) argues: '...of all the causes [of change] the History 13–16 Project was probably the most significant.' He suggests that its philosophy, methodology and pedagogy led a radical shift away from the 'great tradition' of history as a 'received subject' that had dominated teaching for much of the century towards one in which students were 'to do' history not merely receive it.

The 13–16 Project widened the content of history in schools to include contemporary and local dimensions addressing arguments about its relevance. This widening of the subject was continued with the emergence of Women's and Black history and by 1988 HMI argued that history had a particularly important role to play in countering ethnic and gender stereotyping. More importantly, it stressed that history offered something unique to the curriculum and was as a result a 'useful' subject to study. While Sylvester may overestimate the significance of the Project in terms of public examinations (by 1990 only a third of students taking history at GCSE were following SHP syllabuses) it is certainly true that its message found its way into the majority of secondary schools through textbooks and, especially, the *What is History?* pack.

This trend towards 'doing history' was vigorously resisted by, among others, Geoffrey Elton in Ballard (1970, pp.221–30):

> In the current debate...we hear rather more about the manner than the matter...about the various ways in which the study of history can be made more exciting, useful or 'relevant' than about the particular bits of history it is advisable to convey to school children...

The limits for the subsequent debate had been laid down. The problem for new history was the shallowness of its epistemological, pedagogical and 'populist' roots. An emphasis on process and pedagogy could easily become perverted into an emphasis on skills and methods within a framework that was historical, but only in passing.

Between 1975 and 1980 some critique of new history was attempted. Davies and Pritchard (1975) recognised the value of developments since 1968 but still entitled their paper 'History Still in Danger?' Using evidence collected from interviews with prospective student teachers they concluded that

> There is little evidence that the 'new' history has gained ground. Few interviewees talk of skills acquired, but many of the textbooks, dictated notes and learning facts...School history remains essentially content-based, chronologically arranged, nationally-based, politically-oriented, formal in learning method, limited in resources and deficient in attention to both

objectives and their evaluation. (p.114)

In retrospect the extent to which new history led to curriculum reform by the mid-1970s was perhaps more limited than often believed. It did, however, leave a legacy, largely artificial and increasingly caricatured, of a deeply felt division between new and 'old' or traditional history teaching. The already confused direction of the subject in secondary schools was further exacerbated by this increasingly sterile divide, a situation complicated even more by the stridently populist critique of the curriculum as a whole. The critique of new history demonstrated that it was insecurely rooted. Palmer (1976) suggested that the Coltham-Fines taxonomy might have been more effective if fleshed out with curriculum examples and Gard and Lee (in Dickinson and Lee, 1978, pp.21–38) submitted it to a vigorous critique concluding that 'The analysis breaks down partly because it is forced into the procrustean bed of the "objectives" approach...'

The publications of Shemilt (1979, 1980) on the Schools History Project and Rogers (1979) on the practical application of new history brought some empirical detachment to the debate. However, the failure of new history to establish a dominant position in the secondary curriculum can be seen in the changing emphasis of the debate from teaching and learning to justifying the continued presence of the subject in the curriculum. Pedagogy mattered less than survival. Limm (1980, p.25) expressed the widely held belief that 'There comes a time when the questions "what should we teach?" and "how should we teach?" have to be seen to be rooted in a sound rationale for teaching the subject in the first place.' Barker (1981, p.14) argued, taking a populist position, that the defence of history in the 1970s

> ducked the Comprehensive question: How do you involve the ordinary mass of youngsters in the moral, social, political and economic problems at the core of human civilisation?..The nature of History (evidence/deduction) rather than children or learning became the focus of the reform movement...The central problem of creating a common access to a shared past is passed over...

and Jenkins and Brickley (1986) highlighted the current obsession with 'skillology'.

Almost twenty years of debate, largely within the history profession, had achieved very little. The discussions that began as a defence of history against charges of irrelevance and threats of integration, developed into a critique of new history in the mid-1970s and emerged in the 1980s as the need to justify history's place in the secondary curriculum as a response to numerical pressures exerted, in particular, through the option system post-14. The issue had already been politicised but its nature changed irrevocably with the shift in the discussion of the history curriculum as an internal pedagogical issue to one where the initiative moved towards central prescription. In this process, events in 1984–5 played a central role.

Curriculum 11–16 (HMI, 1977, pp.49–52) and *History in the Primary and Secondary Years* (HMI, 1985) provided a clear statement of the history teacher's concerns, placing a distinct emphasis on the values enshrined in new history. Justification lay not in the intrinsic value of the subject but in the skills that could be developed and mastered. This obviously fitted into the emerging instrumental view of the curriculum. Historical skills could be seen as a means to an end, content could not. This was, however, increasingly *not* the view of government, especially after the appointment of Sir Keith Joseph as Secretary of State for Education in 1981. The subsequent debate polarised into conservative, traditional, patriotic and populist history and leftist, radical, new history in a far more public forum than the debate ten years earlier. The debate rumbled on through the remainder of the 1980s. The *Times Educational Supplement* (1984) summed up the situation in an aptly titled editorial '1066 and all that...':

> What stands out is the difference in fundamental objectives between those who see history as a principal ingredient in the formation of a citizen's concept of his country, past and present, and those who see it as a whetstone on which to sharpen critical faculties and power of reasoning.

while *The Times* (26 August 1984), in an editorial entitled, somewhat uninspiringly, 'The Uses of History', concluded that 'It is good to enter adult society with pride in its past. It is better still to come with the beginnings of an understanding of it.'

The issue of managing and learning history had become confused with a predictable concern about a national history. This ritual blood-letting within the profession and consequent failure to get to the heart of the issue has perhaps done more to weaken the case for history in the secondary curriculum than anything else. Statements, like that of Elton at a meeting of The Historical Association in the House of Lords: 'We need more English history...and not this non-existent history of ethnic entities and women...More kings and bishops than wool in the fifteenth century.' (*The Guardian*, 1986) were instantly memorable. In many respects the subsequent extended debate on National Curriculum history and on *The Dearing Report* turned over the same ground ploughed originally in the 1970s and early 1980s. The result, seen in the original National Curriculum Orders for history and in the outcome of the Dearing review, is an uneasy compromise between the traditionalist focus on content and the progressive emphasis on skills. The continuity of the 'great tradition' of history teaching with its emphasis on history as a socialising subject transmitting the culture and shared values of society has been reasserted.

There is a widespread perception that history has been in almost continual danger since the early 1960s and that there has been only limited success in articulating a case for including it in the secondary curriculum, especially post-14. Attempts to base a rationale for history on 'skills', though undoubtedly responsible for a change in teaching emphasis, either failed to take account of or seemed to downgrade 'context', creating a damaging division between traditional content teaching and skills-based learning. Falling rolls and the changing DES and DFE curricular emphases, as well as a failure to achieve a satisfactory synthesis between these two stereotypes, has led to real confusion among many history teachers. The history profession is divided not just on what to do but also on fundamental matters of principle about the nature and function of history in the curriculum.

Managing history in the whole-school curriculum: establishing the parameters

The position of history within the National Curriculum has been a catalogue of decline. Initially there were demands that both history and geography should be part of the foundation curriculum across all key stages. Then students had to opt for either history or geography at Key Stage 4. Finally, *The Dearing Report* removed national testing for the subjects, at least in the short-term, at the end of Key Stage 3 and the obligation for all students to follow either history or geography courses post-14. There has been a gradual, but inexorable, reduction in the position of history and geography within the whole-school curriculum despite the fact that, if GCSE and A level numbers are a valid indication, they are popular with students. The arguments for this process have, to some degree, been persuasive. Teachers argued that the whole-school curriculum was too crowded; that there were too many tests and what was the value of standard assessment tests only at the end of Key Stage 3 when students were likely to have already made their option choices; that the need now existed to provide for vocational courses post-14 via the medium of General National Vocational Qualifications (GNVQ). Taken as a whole, the narrowing of the National Curriculum to the core subjects of mathematics, English and science with short courses in technology and modern languages plus PE and RE has been welcomed by the teaching profession. It has, in effect, led to history being relegated from the

Premier to the Second Division in successive seasons. This leaves the subject very exposed. It is essential for any manager of history to be able to make a case for it both in a collaborative framework within the humanities and more broadly within the whole-school curriculum.

The British Academy was told in July 1988 by Kenneth Baker (DES, 1988a), then Secretary of State for Education, that:

> I am quite clear that every civilised society, to remain civilised, needs to develop in its citizens the aptitudes and intuitions which flow from engagement with the humanities. The humanities are an inter-related effort to give intellectual expression to the significance of what it is to be human.

There is a general consensus that an understanding of the humanities should be part of a core curriculum but its precise nature is, however, far from clear. Is the humanities a subject or a combination of disciplines each with their own distinctive methodologies and substantive content held together by administrative convenience and by their joint involvement in investigating human development in different cultures? In many schools, where the humanities consist of history, geography and religious studies, often with a combination of other subjects like sociology, economics and politics thrown in post-16, it is clear that administrative rather than cultural imperatives are to the fore. While humanities used to be the norm in secondary schools in Years 7 and 8, the logic behind the National Curriculum has resulted in history and geography reappearing in distinct slots in the timetable. History teachers have justifiably asserted their single-subject status with considerable vigour in the last ten years. Many are still equivocal about collaboration because of what history may lose through perceived dilution. The work undertaken through an interdisciplinary or integrated approach has tended to decline as a consequence. At Key Stage 4 the humanities subjects are in direct competition with each other for an often declining number of students.

How can the case for history be buttressed through its position within a collaborative humanities framework? Woff (1991) and Keelan and Dickinson (1991) both make strong cases for the subject within the humanities. Woff argues for the idea of the humanities as an interrelated or integrated approach to the study of particular aspects of human activity. He suggests, however, that it is difficult to see how the continuation of a single subject structure or even co-operation between subject specialists can ensure an adequately coherent learning experience. This is, however, precisely the organisational structure that exists in most schools with either autonomous heads of subjects or heads of subject within a faculty system. Under the National Curriculum it is easier to teach the humanities

8

subjects separately than within the overarching conceptual framework of humanities. Large numbers of teachers appear to have welcomed this trend. It has allowed them to concentrate on consolidating their position as a foundation subject within the first three stages of the National Curriculum. This is a cautious position but not a surprising one as many, especially those who are non-specialists, have been battered and confused by change. Even schools with a strong tradition in the humanities to the end of Key Stage 3 have increasingly abandoned an approach that offered students a broader and more flexible appreciation of themes and areas of experience in favour of the more conservative structures thought necessary for successful learning within the National Curriculum.

This negative, essentially structural argument is countered by Keelan and Dickinson (1991, p.93) who maintain that it is essential to ensure that the best of existing humanities practice is known and considered by policy-makers and teachers of both history and geography. They suggest that

> if teachers of history are to best serve historical values in the coming years then their planning should include careful consideration of how their subject can contribute positively to co-operative schemes, whether they be integrated or modular and called humanities or even 'history/geography'.

We can now extend this into the field of vocational education (Brown, 1994a). The question those managing learning in history need to ask is: what can history bring to a collaborative curriculum that is a unique or a supportive contribution? The dimension of change over time is a central feature of any account of the human and social. The American sociologist C. Wright Mills went so far as to suggest that history 'is and must be, the very shank of social sciences'. An analysis of environmental issues in modern Russia would be meaningless without reference to industrial developments under communism and the economic policies of successive Soviet leaders. The reverse is also true and perhaps the least justifiable intervention by government in the history curriculum was that by Kenneth Clark with his 'thirty year embargo'.

History can also been characterised as a mode of enquiry and it is in this area, perhaps more than in its substantive content, that its contribution to the collaborative curriculum can be seen more clearly. Peter Rogers (1984, p.22) argues that

> What is at stake is the sort of grounds for a valid knowledge claim, and history provides much more reliable grounds for such claims about the past because it embodies and employs the techniques and procedures for identifying and handling evidence that have been refined over time into the best available...

History provides essential procedural frames of reference that have validity across the whole-school curriculum. Its role is not confined to the what and why of the past. The information skills necessary for the successful completion of assignments at, for example, GNVQ Foundation and Intermediate, leave considerable scope for historical methods like the collection and collation of information, the critical examination of information and the communication of conclusions orally and in writing (Brown, 1994a). Being able to enquire and write as well as think historically are essential features of effective learning within the humanities as well as across the whole-school curriculum. It is the failure of many students to identify and appraise sources of information that leads to ineffective and inefficient learning.

The contribution of history to the humanities is multi-faceted and operates at a number of levels. This provides a powerful case for the position of history, and managers of history should exploit the nature of the subject as a central feature in enriching and enlightening the humanities curriculum. This can lead to history in school being put to even more effective use. So if there is a strong case for the contribution of history within the humanities how can it be achieved in practice? Three features of collaborative learning within the humanities need to be considered:

1. Managers need to be clear *why they wish to move in the direction of a collaborative curriculum.* There may be an intellectual argument that the human and social in the curriculum should be delivered through themes or through a developmental series of modules. It is, however, more likely, as Keelan and Dickinson (1991, p.99) suggest, that they are concerned to protect history in the face of a powerful geography tradition or more generally against demands for extended space by the core National Curriculum subjects or the loss of teachers in history. For the manager of history there may be a trade-off between loss of subject autonomy and the achievement of subject security within a humanities structure. Whatever justification is at the heart of the decision it must be both positive and practical in drawing on existing expertise and it must enhance already existing excellence in learning.

2. There must be a recognition and acceptance that collaborative curriculum planning and delivery will *reduce the autonomy* of history and the habit of teachers working more or less alone. The move towards a humanities curriculum will, inevitably, 'open up' the classroom. In the past it was this aspect of the collaborative curriculum in secondary schools that acted as the main deterrent to innovation and curriculum change. Teacher appraisal, changes in initial teacher training and

regular inspection have led to a rapid decline in teachers working in a vacuum behind closed doors.

3. There is, finally, the *management dimension*. A collaborative curriculum requires a team-approach to planning, delivering, monitoring and evaluation. Time needs to be allocated to bring staff together to exchange ideas and experiences. There must be proper financing.

The argument for a collaborative framework for the humanities is perhaps stronger today than it has been for the last decade. It is possible to arrive at this conclusion via a negative route. Collaboration can be seen as a largely defensive and resource-oriented strategy that is administratively convenient and allows for the efficient utilisation of staffing. This has been called a potential defence for a 'rump Humanities' (Haslam, 1986). Alternatively, collaboration can be seen as a positive vehicle for delivering effective learning within the humanities. Collaboration in the curriculum may be seen as the medium to achieve collaboration in management and in teaching and learning. It is here that managers of history should look for a justification for their subject.

Change in education used to mean more of the same only better; the process of incremental change. This has been seen increasingly as an unrealistic approach to change in schools since the past cannot provide the answers. New ideas were necessary to guide practice. The whole-school curriculum is an idea of relatively recent origin for schools grappling with the practicalities of implementing the original National Curriculum. It has, however, proved an effective medium for whole-school improvement. It moved the curriculum debate on structures in schools away from notions of teacher autonomy towards teacher collegiality and collaboration. It has also allowed schools to focus on the learning process and upon student entitlement within a clearly focused curricular agenda. It requires schools to address learning inequalities grounded in gender, ethnic origin and ability that the move to comprehensive organisation had failed to resolve. It is part of the development of a 'consumer' and 'business' led approach to curriculum management. The question that managers of history in secondary schools need to answer is: what is the place of my subject within the whole-school curriculum framework?

We must be clear about the constraints that have prevented history departments contributing to the whole-school perspective. First, the history department is a vested interest (Brown, 1991b). The National Curriculum has, to a significant degree, legitimised this situation with its focus upon the subject as the major vehicle for delivering learning. Yet until the constraints imposed by vested interests are confronted by line-managers there can never be a thorough review of the curriculum and the creation of a new learning vision. It is in the annual competition between departments and faculties for teaching periods, staffing and resources that the malign influence of vested interests is fully exposed. Demands by vested interests do have their place in schools but they should always be viewed as secondary to the demands of the curriculum as a whole. This distinction is at the heart of the matter and it is something that managers of history have to come to terms with in a positive way. If not, vested interests will become a 'consecrated obstacle' to change in schools.

Research suggests that teachers fall into two broad categories:

1. Teachers whose approach is highly individualistic and subject-oriented. These are often, though not always, teachers with considerable experience for whom change is often perceived as a threat. Their concerns are with their subjects and with the 'cult of the practical'.

2. Teachers who have a broader perspective and who adopt collective or collegial or collaborative approaches to the curriculum as a whole.

Both orientations have their place in managing the curriculum. The problem has been that managers in history have often allowed their individualistic role to determine their approach to curriculum planning at the departmental and whole-school levels. The result has been demands for conservation, 'innovation without change' and an often profound failure to address the issues that face departments in the future.

There is no doubt of the importance of subject teaching to student motivation and learning and, in secondary schools, this is reinforced by the centrality of examination results. Work in subjects is often imaginative and innovative but overall it lacks coherence. It lacks a unifying vision within the whole-school learning of students. It is no longer acceptable for schools to introduce a new subject which results in history or any other subject forfeiting some of its time allocation. This 'Dutch auction' approach to curriculum planning – I hesitate to use the word 'planning' in this context – resolves nothing. Traditional innovation theory in schools suggests that successful change cannot occur until teachers are prepared to change. This is a recipe for inertia or, at most, structural change – for what has been called 'innovation without change'. Innovation in business demands an analysis of market potential of projected change. Change is related to improved output. In schools this means pedagogical change leading to an increased recognition of student needs at an individual level and a consequent change in teaching styles as a means to improving learning output. If managers in history are to play their proper role in whole-school developments they have to be prepared to consider innovation techniques in business as a basis for innovation in their departments. These provide a way through traditional educational techniques by emphasising the value of team approaches and the need for clarity of aims and objectives related clearly to outcomes. This will empower managers by creating a market- and client-focused approach to planning.

Heads of department need to resolve the twin issues of vested interest and innovation without change within their own departments before they can contribute effectively to a whole-school curricular perspective (Brown, 1992a). Any process of change, reorganisation or reorientation will inevitably encounter conflict. People do not like change, frequently they do not understand the rationale behind it and consequently they fear it. What is unavoidable is the destabilisation of cherished meanings of self, organisation and service. This loss of legitimacy can be devastating in personal terms for teachers and can trigger a range of deflection techniques, especially the re-assertion of the validity of subject as opposed to whole-school issues. It is the responsibility of the head of department to manage these fears, which are often expressed in attempts to deflect discussion away from the focus on change into peripheral issues. This means giving teachers of history ownership of the changes. The critical question is how?

Initially there will be a high degree of confusion and ambiguity as teachers assert the importance of the *status quo*. The history manager needs to define the fundamental problems and identify those with legitimate interests, especially the key 'influentials' within a department. Purposes, goals, participation, authority, alliances and key issues are then clarified. This demands an audit of needs in human, physical and financial terms, a determination of time scales, the creation of compromises and devising of creative solutions to potential blockages. This is essentially a political process and is perhaps the most painful stage in the process of development. The planning and consultative process proceeds within the agreed negotiating framework. Collegial or confrontational, the detailed planning continues and a new vision emerges that is exciting and is able to raise commitment both individually and collectively. Implementation will lead to modification and adjustment to the agreed plan. There will be crises, some instability, and individual and group bereavement if the previous stages have not been accomplished effectively and have failed to establish ownership. The role of the head of history within the whole-school curriculum parallels the process within the department. The establishment of a collaborative culture within a department, across a faculty and through the whole-school curriculum is essential if individual teachers, departments and schools are to move forward and change.

The case for developing a collaborative culture for history within a department, across the humanities and as part of the whole-school curriculum is a considerable one. It allows the development of 'vision' in the product definition of history and places at a premium the quality delivery of that vision. At the heart of both vision and quality is the developmental or change process. Change as a mechanism is always difficult and challenging to established positions. In schools it is generally controversial and accompanied by conservative posturing and, as a result, it is often aimless and not completed according to an agreed action plan. A collaborative culture grounded in a clear evaluative process is a fundamental part of developmental strategies. If the learning of history is to be managed effectively for the benefit of all students, allowing them to make real progression in their achievement, then the management ethos of a department needs to be clearly defined, expressed articulately and implemented efficiently.

Prioritising history: the management dilemma

An important distinction can be made between specific classroom management tasks and the more general school management role of the head of department. They are both concerned with the achievement of goals through the collaborative efforts of teams of people and the creation of effective organisational means to ensure that educational values, goals and intentions are put into practice. Achieving quality learning is a common objective. There is, however, still a management dilemma that needs to be resolved.

What priority should managers establish for their subject in the whole-school curriculum? It is in addressing this question that the management dilemma becomes most apparent. Should the head of department view issues simply from a history perspective or should that perspective be tempered by an understanding of the broader picture? It cannot be a case of either/or. To manage effectively it is necessary that both perspectives play a part in determining the planning of student learning in history. Much of this book will focus on how these competing pressures can be resolved. Collaborative management – as a means of securing the place of history as a specific subject within the humanities and the whole-school curriculum – is the channel through which a proactive approach to teaching and learning can be achieved. It is collegial and eminently adaptable to changing needs and requirements. It is grounded in four principles:

1. All teachers are managers and should be recognised as such.

2. Management is about people not simply paper. Effective and efficient 'person management' is essential if management structures are to be of tangible value and lead to effective learning.

3. Collaborative management structures and styles are important attributes of effective schools and need to be inherent in any agreed structure.

4. The primary function of schools is to develop effective learning among all students and the primary concern of management must be to create the proper environment in which that may occur. An instructional imperative must be at the heart of management for excellence.

Managers of history have an overriding responsibility to ensure that their management allows students to learn more effectively not only within their subject but also across the whole-school curriculum.

CHAPTER 2

Learning History

We live in an instrumental world where the value of studying a subject is frequently viewed in terms of extrinsic and tangible results rather than its intrinsic worth. In secondary schools heads of history and their staff are accountable internally and externally for public examination grades and National Curriculum attainment targets and now level descriptors. Parents are concerned to know what levels their children are on and how they can move up to the next level or what grades they will achieve in GCSE, GNVQ or A and AS levels. The same applies to students who often ask, especially when opting for history during Year 9 and post-16, what the pass rate is and how studying the subject will allow them to achieve their own objectives. In this situation learning is a means to an end. Although teachers cannot afford to ignore the instrumental imperative, learning history means far more than simply passing examinations.

The development of student learning is at the heart of all departmental management. This chapter will first sketch what it means to learn history: an understanding of recent research on this issue is essential if learning is to be managed effectively by both teacher and student. It then explores the pedagogical and management issues teachers of history need to address if learning is to be both developmental and efficient. In particular gender, race and language will be considered. Finally, the discussion is drawn together and some models for effective learning and teaching are suggested.

What is meant by learning history?

With the exception of English, learning history in schools is one of the most contested areas of the National Curriculum. For some, especially those on the Right, learning history is about students *knowing* the key facts about the past and being able to regurgitate those facts in writing, especially in essays. Here the focus is on knowing *about* the content of history as part of highly politicised arguments concerning national pride and values. Others suggest that learning history is about developing the skills of evidential criticism and the procedural methodology used by historians. This division between content and skills does little to elucidate the nature of learning history in the classroom. It is artificial, certainly something that professional historians would reject and is a reflection of broader social and political concerns than questions of pedagogy.

The discussion of the nature of historical knowledge in Rogers (1979, pp.9–16) is a useful starting-point. He suggests that history, like all forms of knowledge, has three main characteristics from which it gains its coherence. Firstly, there is its propositional character or 'know that'. Secondly, its procedural character or 'know how'. It is the propositional nature of history that is more distinctive and it is based on narrative or the story of the past. This accounts for the argument that students should 'know' the facts. However, Rogers (1979, pp.6–7) maintains that

> Both these distinctive features of a form or type of knowledge are equally important. To 'know' something on good authority means that the proposition which one 'knows' is the outcome of an enquiry which satisfies the appropriate procedural criteria...only 'know how' can give 'the right to be sure' because it is the only valid basis for claims to 'know that'.

The relationship between 'know that' and 'know how' is therefore a symbiotic one and as such 'mere propositions cannot really count as *knowledge* but at best as *information*.' The third distinguishing feature is conceptual. Concepts, many of which come from disciplines other than history, provide the framework without which there can be no real grasp of the propositional and procedural. The problem for teachers is that there is no agreement about key concepts in history. For students to learn history they have to master the propositional, procedural and conceptual dimensions of the subject. This can be represented diagrammatically, as in Figure 2.1:

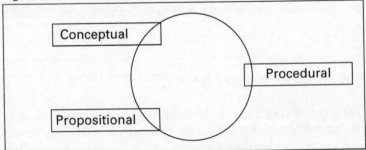

Figure 2.1 The dimensions of learning history

What does this mean in practice? Take, for example, the question of the industrial revolution within Key Stage 3 *Expansion, Trade and Industry*. Teachers need to be clear what propositional, procedural and conceptual issues are raised by the industrial revolution and the structural relationship between them if the learning they intend is to be achieved. Figure 2.2 illustrates the symbiotic nature of their relationship. Why an industrial revolution occurred, central to the propositional, cannot be addressed by students unless they consider the conceptual issues of causation and chronology and the procedural and contested issue of its evidential basis. Skills, concepts and content interact within the historical process. They cannot be separated without fatally damaging student understanding of the past. The effective management of learning history must therefore encompass all three.

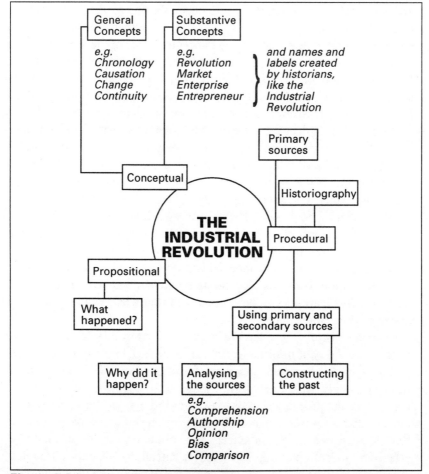

Figure 2.2 Learning dimensions in practice

Shawyer, Booth and Brown (1988) consider how educational research has gradually enhanced our knowledge of how historical understanding develops. This has clearly been influenced by more general works on cognitive development. The Piagetian distinction between different stages of thought led to investigations into children's historical understanding (Jahoda, 1962; Peel, 1967; Hallam, 1970, 1972). The results were disappointing. Children's historical understanding was found to be confused and slow to develop. Hallam (1972), for example, found that strategies designed to encourage 13-year-olds to think at a formal level had little impact. The late 1960s and 1970s saw, largely under the influence of Gagne and Bloom, the behaviourist development of learning hierarchies and taxonomies of objectives. This approach had a limited appeal for most history teachers though it was popularised by Coltham and Fines (1971) and indirectly influenced the emergence of the *Schools Council Project, History 13–16*. However, neither the Piagetian nor behaviourist approaches addressed the central issue of the structure of the subject and how to make it accessible and relevant to young people. Bruner's notion of the 'spiral curriculum' is certainly applicable for history teachers since it recognises the varied ways in which children learn in the classroom. History is not, at least in its content, a developmental subject as, for example, science is, where understanding particular scientific processes is a prerequisite for successful learning. Students can study the Reformation without having a detailed understanding of the nature of the medieval church and Papacy and they can enhance their understanding of the subject by revisiting it at different points in their school lives. In the primary school children may look at Henry VIII in terms of whom he married and what he did. At Key Stage 3 the Reformation might be considered in more detail through a largely factual discussion of what happened and why. Post-16 the complexities of the Reformation from a theological perspective might be explored. In this way student learning is developed and knowledge and conceptual understanding of the subject is increased.

Learning history must have a context (Stanford, 1994). This places history as a 'body of information' at the fore in teaching. Students do need to know what happened and why. It is, however, difficult to equate learning simply with factual knowledge of the subject. Students need conceptual and procedural tools to examine how we construct accounts of the past and organisational and communication skills to convey what they have learned to a wider audience. These allow teachers to evaluate how effective student learning has been. I intend to look at chronology, causation, historiography and evidence, and comment on the now defunct Attainment Targets since I see them as an attempt, albeit flawed, to establish a learning hierarchy of skills in history. I will then comment briefly on the new Level Descriptions for the unitary History Attainment Target.

Concepts, skills and Attainment Targets

Firstly, the issue of *chronology* (Stanford, 1994, pp.182–91). A sense of time, or chronological knowledge and understanding as it is called in the revised History Orders, is fundamental to the study of history and, unlike many of the concepts employed by historians, is largely non-controversial. It does, however, present problems for students, who find it difficult to define and chart its development, and therefore for teachers (Cooper, 1992, pp.28–31). Jahoda (1962) revealed that even adolescent children could only think in terms of a short number of years. Peel (1967) followed up this work with some research on how historical understanding developed and indicated how, with dates and a timeline (drawn carefully to scale), children could think in longer spans. Lally and West (1981) suggested that constant reference to a visual timeline that includes the present is the single most effective way of developing children's sense of historical time. As a tool for developing understanding timelines have a valuable place in teaching but, unless they are contextualised, students may find them confusing and will not make connections between, for example, timelines of the revolution in the textile industry and the life of Richard Arkwright (Hodkinson, 1995; Wood, 1995; Simchowitz, 1995). Having a clear chronology is essential if students are to manage their learning of history effectively, but how are we to evaluate the level of that learning? The National Curriculum Attainment Targets did not specifically deal with chronology although AT1(a): change and continuity Levels 1 and 2 were exemplified in the Orders by: 'L1: place in sequence events in a story about the past' and 'L2: place familiar objects in chronological order'. This implies a low level of learning that does not recognise just how complex and on occasions contentious the construction of chronologies can be for the historian. For example, Level 1 made no real distinction between a teacher listing events on the blackboard and asking students to draw a timeline from them and students reading a text and constructing their own chronology from the information obtained. Yet the former can be a mechanical exercise while the latter requires comprehension of the text as well as the ability to select the relevant information from which to construct a timeline. My own research with Years 8 and 9 students in mixed ability groups over three years indicates that understanding of chronology can be seen in terms of the following progression. It is possible to distinguish the following levels: (a) students can fill in a prepared timeline with information provided by the teacher in chronological order; (b) students can produce a timeline from information provided but not to scale; (c) students can produce a timeline to scale from provided information; (d) students can construct a scaled timeline using information obtained from one text or source; (e) as (d) but with more than one text or source; (f) students can produce timelines on the same topic from several sources and draw connections between them.

Secondly, *causation* (Leff, 1969, pp.58–70; Atkinson, 1978, pp.140–87; Stanford, 1994, pp.194–204). E.H. Carr (1962, p.87) suggests that no one should commit 'the solecism of calling oneself a student of history or a historian who does not recognise that history is the study of causes'. There is no denying the importance of causation as a means of making the significance and sequencing of events intelligible. The problem teachers face is that the search for causes can easily become a mechanical exercise in which students seek C_1, C_2 and C_3 as an explanation for E. Historical explanation arises not as a mechanical search for causes but from the diverse elements that made the situation in question. As Leff (1969, p.69) argued:

> The distinction in terminology is not merely verbal. Cause denotes a relation of antecedent to consequent which...is rarely attainable, temporally or logically, in human events. Factor or element allows the full play of events, long-term and short-term, foreseeable and unforeseen, without seeking to reduce them to a linear order, which is the assumption of all causal explanation.

This sophistication is, however, often difficult to achieve in the classroom. Early results from the CHATA Project (Concepts of History and Teaching Approaches at Key Stages 2 and 3) suggest that students progress through the following stages of historical understanding (Dickinson and Lee, 1994, pp.88–96): a *baffling past* where the past may arouse student interest when they encounter it but which they probably do not see any reason to explain and which they certainly cannot explain; a *'divi' past* where students do not assume any need to find out about the particular values and beliefs of people in the past and view them as intellectually and morally inferior; an *ignorant past* where students assume that the behaviour of people in the past is to be seen, not as stupid but rather as something to be explained in terms of their 'not being as clever as us' and being hindered by what they cannot yet do; *generalised stereotypes* where students assume that people in the past were very much like those today and that actions can be understood by reference to a 'conventional' or stereotypical account of people's intentions, values and goals; *everyday empathy* where students assume that there is a point in empathising with people in the past but suppose that their actions were very much the same as those of people today; *restricted historical empathy* where students argue that we must understand the past by reference to evidence of the specific situations in which people found themselves; and finally *contextual historical empathy* where students place their understanding of actions in the past in a wider context of contemporary beliefs, values and material conditions and differentiate between these and those that are prevalent today. The nature of progression in Attainment Target 1(b) was certainly mechanistic. Level 3 asked students to give 'a reason' for an event or development while in the next level students had to show that events have 'more than one cause and consequence'. The development of an understanding of causation – from mono-causal explanations (Level 3) to interpretations in which causes were recognised as of varying importance (Level 6), were linked together (Level 7) and the relative importance of linked causes was recognised (Level 8) – seems, however, to correspond to how students learn.

Thirdly, *historiography*. Attainment Target 2 was the most contested, yet perhaps the most innovative, of the methods for evaluating learning put forward in the History Orders (Harper, 1993; McAleavy, 1993; Scott, 1994). Carr (1962, p.22) argued that

> the facts of history never come to use 'pure', since they do not and cannot exist in a pure form: they are always refracted through the mind of the recorder. It follows that when we take up a work of history, our first concern should be not with the facts which it contains but with the historian who wrote it.

The problem for students and teachers is that while there is an objective past there can be no objective history (Jenkins, 1991, 1995). Since historians lack the means of testing what happened empirically they can, as Christopher Blake (1959, p.339) suggested, only 'recreate reality on paper'. This does not mean that historians do not want to find the truth about the past using the available sources. However, the truth for a historian today becomes an interpretation for a succeeding generation. If there cannot be one, true, history but only different histories of the past it is important to ask how far AT2 could develop this understanding in students. The major problem with AT2 was that it contained three potential progression routes:

- *Route 1*: helped students to distinguish between fact and opinion, myth and reality, and covered Levels 1, 3 and 5.

- *Route 2*: concerned the reasons why there are different interpretations of the past and covered Levels 4, 6, 8 and 9.

- *Route 3*: helped students to evaluate interpretations of the past and covered Levels 7 and 10.

It is far more difficult to establish a hierarchy for student learning as a result. Work with thirty Year 9 top set students on four different interpretations of the slave trade in *Expansion, Trade and Industry* showed clearly the nature of the problem. All students were able to achieve Level 3 distinguishing between 'facts' and 'point of view', but only six students were able to recognise that these interpretations may have differed from what is known to have happened (Level 5). However, over half the students were able to achieve Level 8, showing effectively from the sources that attitudes and events can influence an individual's interpretation of the past. For example, how and why a modern black historian's perspective of the slave trade was different from that of a Victorian historian. Four students achieved Level 10 showing an appreciation of the need for objectivity by historians but, as one wrote:

> It isn't a case of an objective truth but of an objective use of the sources available. The black historian thinks, like me, that slavery was wrong and immoral but what he tries to do, using the sources, is to explain why it happened and tries to understand it.

Learning AT2 was not therefore a simple progression up the levels but a complex, spiralling appreciation and mastery of the three different routes.

Finally, the question of *primary evidence* (Stanford, 1994, pp.133–66). The use of primary evidence is now a commonplace in classrooms and this might suggest that there would be fewer pedagogical problems. This is far from being the case. The use of sources has been regarded as the cornerstone of new history and has consequently been accepted by many teachers as 'a good thing' and as a central model for good teaching and learning. This is unfortunate and often untrue. Learning in which sources play a pivotal role can become exercises devoid of context, essentially concerned with comprehension and divorced from developing an understanding of the past. It is not enough that historians use sources, teachers need to pay close and critical attention to how they are used.

The major problem teachers and students have with primary evidence is that the ability to learn from the sources requires a multi-layered conceptual approach. All sources as texts, whether written, visual or oral, have to be read and comprehended. Without this students cannot go forward to consider concepts like context, authorship, judgement, opinion, bias or prejudice, all of which are essential if the reliability and validity of an individual source are to be evaluated. And all this before comparisons can be made between sources. This creates significant problems for evaluating how effective learning has been and for the management of learning using sources. Shemilt's evaluation (1980) suggested that, while Schools History Project students were far less inclined than his control students to view the 'facts' of history as certain, they did find the concept of evidence difficult. Shemilt (1986) distinguished four levels of thinking about evidence: (a) 'evidence = information'; (b) evidence gives answers to be 'unearthed'; (c) historians work things out and evidence presents problems; and, (d) the context of evidence needed to establish historicity. While these levels may be of value as a diagnostic tool and certainly took the debate on sources significantly forward, they do not provide a sufficiently sophisticated way of evaluating the extent of student learning.

Did Attainment Target 3 take the debate forward? In one sense it did by providing a tentative framework for progression in learning. There was, for example, an obvious progression from Level 5 'comment on the usefulness of a historical source by reference to its content, as evidence for a particular enquiry' and Level 6 'compare the usefulness of different sources as evidence for a particular enquiry'. However, like Shemilt and other researchers, the attainment target treated evidence as a single concept rather than as a sometimes uncomfortable association of diverse ideas. Students may well be able to distinguish between information in a particular source that is broadly factual from opinions expressed by its author but this does not mean that they can make deductions from that source. Evidence from the Schools History Project shows that students do not always transfer their ability to use evidence from Paper 1 to Paper 2. GCSE Examiners' Reports clearly demonstrate that, in other concepts like chronology and causation, many students, even the more able, do not get beyond the stage of 'source = information'. Dickinson and Lee (1985) and Thompson (1985) have, however, explored pedagogy as well as materials and outcomes and commented on the importance of students being able to articulate their difficulties so that they can discuss them and so that the teacher knows what additional information or explanations are needed at a particular time. This suggests a complex interplay between the different ideas that make up learning history using evidence.

Level Descriptions as a means of judgement

The Level Descriptions of the revised History Order are designed to enable student learning to be summarised and reported at particular times, for example, at the end of a year or key stage. They furnish an overview of the key features of typical performance at that level and provide a basis for reaching judgements about student achievement. There are eight levels with the introduction of the notion of 'exceptional performance' replacing the old Levels 9 and 10. It is made very clear that they should not be seen as teaching and learning objectives. This marks a significant shift away from the assessment-led character of the earlier History Orders. The critical question history teachers need to address is whether they permit progression in learning to be clearly identified. This is difficult to answer as Level Descriptions are supposed to be read as single statements of learning achieved. There is generally progression between one level and the next but without breaking each description level down into its component parts this is difficult to evaluate effectively.

Table 2.1 sets out the Level Descriptions of the revised History Order. As far as *'factual knowledge'* is concerned there is progression between Level 3 and Level 4 with the critical difference between demonstrating 'factual knowledge' to the Level 4 demonstrating 'factual knowledge and understanding of events, people and changes...' The progression here is presumably one of understanding. If this is the case then Level 5 with its focus on 'increasing depth of factual knowledge and understanding' can be explained through its emphasis on demonstrating factual knowledge across programmes of study rather than simply in one area. Level 6 is concerned with 'making links' between different aspects of the factual knowledge in relation to programmes of study. Level 7 develops the idea of 'links' by differentiating between the outline and detailed components of programmes of study. If progression in factual knowledge means that students will be able to deal with and make links between a growing body of factual content then it could be argued that Levels 3 to 8 do provide a degree of learning progression.

As for the issue of *'chronology and change'*, Level 3 establishes the base for secondary students and suggests that understanding of chronology is 'increasing' and that students can divide the past into different periods of time. In addition, there is 'recognition of some similarities and differences between these periods'. By Level 4 students should be sufficiently developed to make 'use of relevant dates and terms'. The precise meaning of this is not made clear but one must presume that it implies chronological and conceptual awareness to produce 'structured accounts'. At Level 5 students have to 'describe different aspects of past societies' but then it states that students should 'begin to make links between them'. There is a gradual progression in understanding across Levels 6 to 8 from making links to analysing the relationship between events, people and changes.

LEVEL	FACTUAL KNOWLEDGE	CHRONOLOGY, CHANGE AND COMMUNICATION	CAUSATION	UNDERSTANDING HISTORIANS	USING SOURCES
LEVEL 3	Pupils demonstrate factual knowledge of some of the main events, people and changes drawn from the appropriate programme of study.	Pupils show their understanding of chronology by their increasing awareness that the past can be divided into different periods of time, their recognition of some similarities and differences between these periods and their use of dates and terms.	They are beginning to give a few reasons for and results of the main events and changes.	They identify some of the different ways in which the past is represented...	...They find answers to questions about the past by using sources of information in ways that go beyond simple observation.
LEVEL 4	Pupils demonstrate factual knowledge and understanding of aspects of the history of Britain and other countries drawn from the Key Stage 2 or Key Stage 3 Programme of Study.	They use this to describe the characteristic features of past societies and periods and to identify changes within and across periods.	They describe some of the main events, people and changes. They give some reasons for, and results of, the main events and changes.	They show how some aspects of the past have been represented in different ways.	They are beginning to select and combine information from sources.

Table 2.1 Level Descriptions in the revised Order

LEVEL	FACTUAL KNOWLEDGE	CHRONOLOGY, CHANGE AND COMMUNICATION	CAUSATION	UNDERSTANDING HISTORIANS	USING RESOURCES
LEVEL 5	Pupils demonstrate an increasing depth of factual knowledge and understanding of aspects of the history of Britain and other countries drawn from the Key Stage 2 and Key Stage 3 Programme of Study.	They use this to describe and to begin to make links between different features of past societies and periods. They describe events, people and changes... They select and organise information to produce structured work making appropriate use of dates and terms.	They describe and make links between relevant reasons for, and results of, events and changes.	They know that some events, people and changes have been interpreted in different ways and suggest possible reasons for this.	Using their knowledge and understanding, pupils are beginning to evaluate sources of information and identify those that are useful for particular tasks.
LEVEL 6	Pupils use their factual knowledge and understanding of the history of Britain and other countries drawn from the Key Stage 3 Programme of Study to describe past societies and periods and...	...to make links between features within and across periods...They select, organise and deploy relevant information to produce structured work making appropriate use of dates and terms.	They examine and are beginning to analyse the reasons for, and results of, events and changes.	Pupils describe, and are beginning to explain, different historical interpretations of events, people and changes.	Using their knowledge and understanding, they identify and evaluate sources of information which they use critically to reach and support conclusions.

Table 2.1 (Cont'd)

LEVEL	FACTUAL KNOWLEDGE	CHRONOLOGY, CHANGE AND COMMUNICATION	CAUSATION	UNDERSTANDING HISTORIANS	USING SOURCES
LEVEL 7	Pupils make links between their outline and detailed factual knowledge of the history of Britain and other countries drawn from the Key Stage 3 Programme of Study.	They use this to analyse relationships between features of a particular period or society…They select, organise and deploy relevant information to produce well–structured narratives, descriptions and explanations making appropriate use of dates and terms.	They analyse reasons for, and results of, events and changes.	They explain how and why different historical interpretations have been produced.	Pupils are beginning to show independence in following lines of enquiry, using their knowledge and understanding to identify, evaluate and use sources of information critically. They are beginning to reach substantiated conclusions independently.
LEVEL 8	Pupils use their outline and detailed factual knowledge and understanding of the history of Britain and other countries drawn from the Key Stage 3 Programme of Study to…	…analyse the relationship between events, people and changes and between the features of past societies…They select, organise and deploy relevant information…making appropriate use of dates and terms.	Their explanations and analyses of, reasons for, and results of, events and changes are set in their wider historical context.	They analyse and explain different historical interpretations and are to make links between features within them.	Drawing on their historical knowledge and understanding, they use sources of information critically, carry out enquiries about historical topics and independently reach substantiated conclusions.

Table 2.1 (Cont'd)

'*Causation*' is a much easier concept in which to show progression and the Level Descriptions reflect this. In Level 3 students will 'begin' to identify reasons and results; in Level 4 'describe...some events and developments'; in Level 5 'begin to describe and make links between relevant reasons for...' while in Level 6 students 'examine and are beginning to analyse the reasons for...' In Levels 7 and 8 students first 'analyse reasons for...' and then 'explanations and analyses....set in their wider historical context'. There is a degree of progression here for students in terms of how they adduce causation (description to explanation), the frequency of identification and the degree of student autonomy evident.

'*Understanding historians*' is the equivalent of the contentious AT2. It is significant and, in many respects, surprising, that this has been left in. Progression is perhaps most obvious in this area. Level 3 indicates that students should 'identify some of the different ways in which the past is represented' leading into Level 4 where they have to be able to 'show how some aspects of the past have been represented'. A qualitative progression moves things to Level 6 with the substitution of 'suggest possible reasons for this'. Level 6 allows students to begin explaining different historical interpretations and this is developed in Levels 7 and 8 by an increasing critical and judgmental sophistication of student response.

'*Using sources*' is concerned with selecting information from sources and using it. The nature of 'sources' is not made clear but it is possible to assume that it means primary evidence since historiographical material is dealt with earlier in the Level Descriptions.

This brief discussion of whether the Level Descriptions allow for effective progression to be measured suggests that there are problems of consistency across and between levels. There are major problems with the Level Descriptions for the teacher in the classroom who is trying to assess the learning of students. The Descriptions themselves are dense containing a variety of learning experiences. This makes them difficult assessment tools. Breaking them down into their component parts suggests that there are still some difficulties with the progression routes established in some areas of learning. The imposition of a pedagogical unity on the Attainment Target does not reflect how students learn history in any meaningful way. For all their defects the three old Attainment Targets provided a better means for teachers to assess the learning of their students.

The ability of students to learn history is a complex interplay of concepts (some historical, others not), content, methodology, language and pedagogy. Failure in any one of these areas will inevitably limit the extent to which successful learning can occur. It may be possible to identify a hierarchy of learning in history as a diagnostic tool and as a means for assessment, but there is no necessary correlation between, for example, the expertise or confidence to handle the concepts of chronology and causation. History teachers are still far from clear about what successfully learning history means to students (Downey and Levstik, 1991). We are, however, far clearer about the circumstances that can limit that success.

Achieving progression

Heads of History are primarily concerned that their students should be successful in their learning at whatever level. To achieve this they need to be aware of the conditions that may limit that success (Kyriacou, 1986, 1991). Some of these are beyond the control of the secondary school teacher. Students come from primary schools with considerably different experiences and levels of ability in, for example, functional literacy and numeracy. They are at different levels of maturity. They come from different social and environmental backgrounds. Schools can take these differences into account but they cannot nor should they be expected to eliminate them. There are, however, several areas where history teachers can have an influence on the levels of learning that their students can achieve. The problem is that present practice in each area generally has adverse effects on how history is taught and learned. There is also interplay between the different areas that require history teachers to take a holistic view rather than a pragmatic and piecemeal approach.

Gender

Much has been written on the place of women in the past in the history curriculum and the development of GCSE and the National Curriculum has given greater representation and value to the experience of women (Bourdillon, 1988, 1994). Students are now expected to learn about women in the past as part of the National Curriculum. Texts used for Key Stage 3 still show a white, male interpretation of the place of women in the past. The curriculum is still dominated by the actions of men. The primary focus of this section, however, is to consider the potential impact of recent findings about the learning of girls and boys, to suggest possible strategies to alleviate gender inequalities in the history classroom and to enable effective learning by both sexes (Brown, 1992c, 1994b). The manager of history must start by considering the validity of the following widely held perceptions.

Firstly, achievement is not natural and the degree to which individual students, irrespective of gender or race, succeed depends on the extent to which they have taken up the conventions that operate in schools. Competitively based achievement is likely to favour the sex that is more socialised into competition. The social construction, values attached and competitiveness of achievement have had a negative effect on girls (Licht and Dwerck, 1987). There is, however, recent evidence from the University of Minnesota which suggests that teachers need to reconsider this view and that it is boys rather than girls who are disadvantaged because of their limited communicative skills.

Secondly, the selection of what constitutes 'school knowledge' has not only a historical and philosophical base, but also a social, cultural and political one. What the curriculum excludes from its subject matter and where it ranks that subject matter in an evaluative hierarchy have profound social consequences. Mathematical and scientifically based areas of knowledge, involving rationality and high levels of abstraction, have historically been construed as relevant to what might be called the 'public sphere'. They certainly have a primary position in much government thinking. They have also been construed as masculine and falsely regarded as more difficult. Subjects that involve more personal, social, communicative and affective modes of thought are seen as more relevant to the 'private sphere' and gendered as feminine. Arguably, history spans both spheres: it certainly has an important public dimension yet many of the skills required for effective study – communicative skills, for example – have been gendered as feminine. Again this perception must now been viewed in the context of the post-industrial economy in which communicative skills have a far higher profile than in the past, so favouring girls against boys.

Finally, what constitutes learning in society is also important. Historically our society valued lone intellectual learning at the highest levels. As a result learning that is seen as collaborative, negotiated and engaging personal perspectives has often not been regarded as having a high status. Girls are not socialised as autonomous enquiring beings in the ways that boys are. The result of this is that boys' and girls' learning behaviours are likely to be different and boys are more likely to be judged as actual or potential real learners than are girls. This too is now questionable. Collaborative, communicative skills are increasingly more highly prized than lone intellectual activity and this too favours girls. History is certainly a subject in which girls do learn effectively. It is a popular option choice post-14: of those who opt for history about 60 per cent are girls. As a literary subject in which communication skills are fundamental this should not be surprising.

Gender differences do lead to gendered learning or gender-determined outcomes in the classroom. The Minnesota research shows clearly that by the beginning of Key Stage 3 girls have a clear advantage over boys in effective learning if only because their learning is more advanced. It also suggests that there is little that can be done to narrow the learning gap between the two sexes by this stage. This marks a fundamental shift from the previously held view that boys catch up with girls during their secondary school years. Ten years ago teachers were concerned with how they could ensure that girls performed effectively in history. Today we have increasingly to ask that question about boys. So how can we manage history lessons effectively so that successful learning can occur for both sexes? History teachers can mitigate the effects of gender in two different ways: by developing teaching environments that recognise and counter the different experiences of boys and girls and by paying close attention to the ways in which interaction occurs in the classroom.

The teaching environment and gender

Firstly, the way in which the history classroom is laid out carries messages about the kind of behaviour expected in it. Boys and girls tend to occupy these spaces differently. Boys generate a greater presence, whatever the layout, through their body language, their way of moving into seats, the spread of their belongings and their leaning back on chairs. Girls generate more 'enclosed' spaces. They frequently sit under the line of vision of teachers at the front of the class or, where rooms are organised in blocks of tables, in the most peripheral locations. Centre stage is still likely to be occupied by boys. While distribution patterns are not the same in every classroom, nearly all classroom layouts become more or less 'gender marked' and this has consequences for boys' and girls' learning. Where students sit is not as arbitrary as we may think, it can affect the amount and quality of attention individuals receive and reinforce particular levels of confidence or dominance. So what can teachers do in practice about room layout?

It is useful to draw a plan of the classroom and plot how the space is or can be occupied, including what marks the teacher's space. Think about this classroom space in relation to gender. Corners and edges may become gendered zones but can be removed by rearranging tables to create a semi-circular space. In fixed environments where layout cannot be changed easily, how far does the teacher's usual 'marked position' determine the learning space and what are the effects of changing it? In practice students sitting alphabetically can break down space and so develop learning between boys and girls. Research with two Year 10 mixed ability history groups, one sitting alphabetically and the other in single sex groups, found that over a period of four weeks girls in the former group were more willing to answer questions in class that in the latter (53 responses compared to 39). Boys, however, still took the lead in responding (113 compared to 129) though the quality of their answers was more variable than the girls. The result of this was a policy decision in favour of alphabetical seating.

Secondly, display, which is also a vehicle for social messages about the kinds of activities and purposes expected of a room. Girls and boys may well react to this differently. Concerns about displays focus on the content of images and how far they reflect positive images of women. There has been considerable impetus in producing images of women in history. There are certain elements in a room's appearance that teachers cannot change and the degree to which any one teacher can have 'ownership' of a room depends on individual circumstances and requires important management decisions by the head of department. Teachers need to recognise that 'gender appeal' can significantly influence student perceptions of a 'subject matter' and how far that subject matter is 'for them'. Heads of history need to ensure that displays are examined and changed regularly and that the purpose of the display, its potential audiences and student ownership are made explicit. Teachers need to consider what kind of ethos and image of a subject is being generated by the displays in their rooms.

Finally, there are tasks or activities. What is at issue here is the effect different tasks have on the 'feel' of the learning environment for boys and girls and how this influences their approach to learning history. There are likely to be gender differences in preferences for, confidence in, and general appeal of, different tasks that teachers need to take account of and contest. Girls are more likely than boys to prefer and have confidence in less public activity, like personal reading and writing. They may, however, feel more open to scrutiny than boys when these activities are made public. Girls are more likely than boys to appreciate writing as a developmental task, involving drafting processes; boys tend to avoid these processes and feel that they have no use for them. This reflects a recognition by girls of the importance of effective communication in history. In two Year 11 groups three GCSE assignments formed the coursework component. Students were expected to hand in drafts of work for comment and revision. While most boys handed in a first draft and final copy, this applied to only a third of the girls. The remainder of the girls handed in at least two drafts before final copy and 30 per cent handed in three drafts or more before the final copy. Discussions with the students after they had completed the three tasks showed clearly that the girls saw drafting and redrafting as effective means of improving their overall score but also reflected higher levels of commitment to quality learning.

Tasks involving the use of equipment, especially computers, used to develop into boy-dominated activities. In mixed groups boys were often to be seen at the controls of the equipment. This has been explained in the following way. Equipment-centred tasks have a greater publicness about them that can add to girls' inhibitions. Some tasks involved students working together and adopting work roles within the group. In mixed groupings, girls tended to occupy the 'maintenance' roles and boys the 'directive' roles or, if in a minority, an unofficial saboteur role. Decision-making tended to be taken over by the boys, while girls attempted to keep the group to the task. This view of the male monopoly of new technologies has changed dramatically in the past five years. There is little difference between the technical abilities of boys and girls to use computers as an aid to historical learning. There is, however, a marked difference in the ways boys and girls tend to use computers to process information. Girls appear to use computers as a means of achieving answers to historical questions or as a medium through which they can communicate more effectively. Boys, by contrast, take far longer to progress from the 'computer as technology' to the 'computer as a creative learning tool'.

These are some of the activities which indicate that tasks are not neutral contributors to the classroom environment and its gender interaction patterns. So can anything be done about this? Firstly, there needs to be variety. It is not unusual for one history activity to occupy a lesson with no change of learning style required. If this is repeated from lesson to lesson, students soon build up fixed notions of a subject matter and patterns of behaviour to go with it, that can entrench gender perceptions. It is important therefore to vary activities. Secondly, timing and change of pace. Teachers may set the timing of activities at the beginning of a lesson, without building in planned interventions to change the time and pace of tasks. This can have gendered effects. Girls often conscientiously go through the stages, with greater or lesser confidence, depending on the activity, but boys may take short cuts to create time for themselves, allowing them often to sit back and occupy space. This may reflect higher levels of learning by girls than boys, with getting the work done, albeit at a superficial level, as the priority for boys. Thirdly, unplanned or insufficiently communicated time-scales for tasks tend to increase gender differences in behaviour and the dominance of the environment by boys. It allows them to control the time agenda. Teachers need to plan the different stages of lessons with gender in mind and to communicate clearly each step, its time and pace, beforehand and during the lesson.

Finally, balancing tasks between genders. If decisions on who does what in group situations are left generally to the students, the likelihood of inequalities in power is increased. It is important to redress this imbalance. This means: clearly explaining the nature of the student collaboration and giving guidelines on group roles; allocating a specific role to each student in the group; allocating more powerful roles to girls and intervening on turn-taking where there is evidence of male dominance; and nominating one or two students to monitor who does what in groups and discussing the power dimensions of groups with students.

Interaction in the classroom

Interaction in the classroom between teachers and students and between students is varied, continual, dispersed and simultaneous. How teachers manage those interactions in history is important since they can reinforce the ways in which boys and girls learn and the limitations on that learning.

Talk is the key interactive process in classrooms and it is difficult to consider talk apart from teacher-student and student-student interrelations. However, a few comments about its qualities in relation to gender are necessary. Boys talk more than girls, contrary to popular myth. Their actual utterances tend to be shorter than girls', but they occur more often and with fewer pauses. Boys' talk is more 'product'- and information-oriented. It is more inclined to be directive, as opposed to girls' talk which is more extensive but contains more pauses and cues to the listener and is generally more oriented towards attitudes, feelings and social dimensions. Teacher talk in classrooms is goal-directed and task-related and it is public and authority laden. It is therefore more appropriate for boys than girls. Given that classroom talk focuses on goals and tasks establishing a framework for exchanges that moves the task on, – direction rather than reflection – a mode of talking that keeps tight control over the linguistic space favours boys rather than girls. However, girls appear to communicate in history more effectively than boys.

While this mode of talking is characterised by efficiency, there are questions about its effectiveness as a mode of learning. Research, especially in history, suggests that talk is more effective as a learning device if people are given time and space to collect their thoughts and speak, if the emphasis is on explanation and processes rather than result, if it is co-operative and adaptive to responses rather than closed (Dickinson and Lee, 1984).

A considerable amount of research has been conducted on teacher-student interactions on gender with a significant agreement on results.

Teachers interact significantly more with boys than with girls: more than 70 per cent of teacher attention has been recorded. Observations in Manchester as part of the Training History Teachers' Project (1985–7) found that student teachers in Years 7–10 directed more questions to boys than to girls; responded more to boys' hand-raising, calling out or interrupting to answer than to girls'; gave boys more feedback in terms of prompting, clarifying and elaborating on their answers or comments; directed closed questions to girls and gave less expansive forms of feedback; initiated more interactions with boys than with girls and responded to the greater number of student-initiated interactions that come from boys; gave less behaviour criticism to girls, but were more likely to criticise girls for academic performance and incorrect answers; and reprimanded boys and girls in different ways, tending to give 'harder', more aggressive but shorter rebukes to boys and more 'appealing' but often longer ones to girls. Observations as part of teacher appraisal (1991–3) found the same pattern replicated among experienced teachers of both sexes.

These general points do, however, need to be qualified in important respects. Firstly, what concerns teachers most about boys is their behaviour and the demands made on them to control it. The result is that many of their interactions with boys are in the form of discipline contacts. Secondly, teachers' interactions with coloured and black boys, especially those categorised as low achievers, are more negative than those with white boys. Thirdly, when girls are younger they initiate more contacts with teachers than boys to seek approval. As girls get older, this assurance-seeking contact declines: for black girls this occurs earlier than with white girls, suggesting that the former more quickly fail to achieve positive results from these contacts.

Explaining why teachers in the history classroom interact differently with boys and girls is an important question but is very difficult to answer. They may direct more questions to boys to keep them interested, in which case it can be seen as a form of control, or because they seem more interested. Responding to boys' answers may occur because boys, who are highly competitive, are more urgent and persistent, and this urgency of response can be seen as 'keeping things going' and moving the subject matter along. Teachers may give more elaborate comments to boys who enter into the public arena of question and answer with greater confidence and seem to respond to it more positively. More closed questions are directed to girls because publicly girls may be seen as dealing less successfully with open-ended questions.

Given this, it is not surprising that boys receive so much more attention and classrooms can be seen to advantage boys. It is important to recognise that teachers do not directly *cause* this unequal distribution of power in the classroom. Teachers, because of the nature of teaching, learning and classrooms and the gender predisposition within them, interact with this power dynamic and by those interactions can reinforce it, to a greater or lesser extent. This needs to be recognised by teachers and contested in their teaching if girls are to achieve equitable treatment in the history classroom.

Many of the behaviours, situations and events to which teachers respond stem from student-student interaction. Boys are more aggressive and physical in their interactions with each other but also with girls. These interactions can also be highly competitive. Some boys persistently humiliate girls by remarking on their appearance and sexuality. A great deal of boys' behaviour towards girls is sexual harassment, though it is often not recognised as such. Added to this, girls do not often complain. They frequently act with deference towards boys or laugh it off: to do otherwise risks further humiliation. Boys tend to 'put each other down': an expression of their competitiveness. Boys seem to be gendered into continually proving their masculinity in terms of physical strength and aggression, prowess at sport and resistance to displays of emotions and feelings. This can result in intolerance to boys who appear not to conform to this masculine ethos. The consequence is often name-calling and more overt forms of bullying. Boys also have to affirm their superiority over girls. This occurs through various types of humiliation boys inflict on girls, that 'control' girls into subordinate positions.

It is important to recognise that this occurs as a result of gendered characteristics rather than *individual* qualities. Gender factors mean that boys and girls are caught in a dilemma of gain and loss. Girls are ascribed gender positions of being helpful, supportive, co-operative rule-followers. It is therefore against the 'gender grain' to compete with boys on boys' terms. The result is that girls are inclined to adopt alternative modes of behaviour that tend to confirm their social subordination, in the eyes of boys if not in terms of their ability to learn.

What does all this suggest for history teachers and their role in relation to student interaction? The interaction of boys with each other clearly suggests that they are more positively responsive than girls to competition and individualism – which are factors of achievement in schools. A climate that stresses these factors is likely to reinforce boys' learning and undermine girls'. The development of more co-operative learning situations advantages girls *but* boys need to acquire the skills to help them establish and work within them. It is possible for the history teacher to manage student interaction to enable effective learning to occur in the following ways. Group work can be structured as group work, with clearly assigned, even nominated student roles and tasks towards achieving a group goal. This means designing tasks and selecting group roles, especially for boys, on the basis of what skills they can offer the group, as a group. Group work can dissolve into its component individuals doing their own work as this reinforces the position of boys. Talk between students can also be structured by tasks that specifically require students to listen to each other and take turns in speaking. This requires more precision than the usual 'discuss and report back' approach. Other activities, where talk is not necessarily the main focus, can be approached in the same way.

Some conclusions

The gender dynamics of history classrooms are very tentative and recent research has made them even more so. The suggestions made above focus deliberately on changing and improving the conditions of learning in an attempt to give boys and girls equal opportunity to succeed. A recognition by history teachers of why students act as they do and that behaviour has gender implications is the first step in devising strategies that ensure equality of learning opportunity in the classroom. Simply changing what we teach in the history curriculum so that the role of women in the past has a more dominant position is a necessary but hardly sufficient way of providing this. It must be accompanied by how we teach if it is to result in changed attitudes, aspirations and levels of achievement.

Multicultural issues

Many of the issues, in terms of content and pedagogy, that apply to gender issues apply with equal force to multicultural education (see Klein, 1993, for a good general introduction to the issue of race). History teachers challenge stereotyping and prejudice through their analysis of the nature and values of societies past and present and are concerned to improve quality of learning through an awareness of the debilitating effects of the socialisation process. There is no educational reason why students from ethnic minorities should not be able to learn effectively in history any more than why girls should not learn as effectively as boys in the subject. Underachievement may contribute to a vicious circle of teacher and student perceptions and expectations about the performance of particular ethnic minority groups. However, such racism in school is unlikely to be a major influence on attainment when compared to the operation of racism in society generally.

The debate on the question of multicultural education in history often gets bogged down in discussions about content of the curriculum and whether students should study non-European civilisations. McGovern

(1994), for example, asks the following questions about the history proposals developed as a consequence of the Dearing Review:

> Is it really possible to justify a legitimate government interest in the teaching of non-European history? Does Benin, for example, really deserve a place on a prescribed list in the new proposals?..Why should non-European history be compulsory while most of the major European landmarks are optional? Surely, the Roman Empire, the Crusades, the Renaissance and Reformation, the French and Russian Revolutions, are of a higher priority for British children than Asian or African history?

Pankhania (1994, pp.148–9), by contrast, suggests that '...the National History Curriculum attempts to teach students a limited history, a history that does not threaten the British social order with its unequal race, gender and class relations.' Questions about the balance between the respective contents of British, European and world history are important since they convey overt messages about what is of value in British society. They do, however, miss the important pedagogical point of teachers aiming to manage effective learning for all students and combating racism in the classroom. So how can the history teacher ensure that all students, irrespective of ethnic origin, learn effectively?

How much students learn in history depends largely on two things. Firstly, how motivated are they by what they are being taught? This question suggests that the content of history courses is important and is directly relevant to the degree to which students are motivated. It is, however, far from being conclusively shown that students from an Asian background are any more motivated by Asian history than they are by British history. Heads of department need to ensure that those areas of the National Curriculum over which they have some control do take account of the ethnic origins of their students. Secondly, and far more importantly, how much are they taught? It is the way in which teachers teach that, above all, enables students to achieve higher levels of learning in history. Even if teachers do equalise the amount of time given to students from ethnic minorities and students who are white, they may often fail to deliver a quality of teaching most suited to their ethnic minority students' learning styles. Authoritarian teaching styles heighten inequality between the teacher and the student whereas research in the learning of history shows that listening to children, not just talking to them, hugely facilitates their learning (Dickinson and Lee, 1984). The main question that heads of history need to ask about their current practice is: in what ways has this changed to take account of accommodating the multi-racial nature of Britain? It is still common to find history departments (including those with or without ethnic minority students) whose curriculum and teaching strategies appear to be little or no different than they would have been had the debate concerning the need to prepare *all* students for a multi-racial society never taken place.

Language and history

The ability to communicate effectively in English is crucial to the success of all students. This is particularly the case in history (Edwards, 1978), which is an eminently literary subject and makes rigorous linguistic demands on its students. Language in history teaching has two dimensions. Firstly, there is the question of the particular language of the subject. Secondly, there is the question of how history can make a contribution to the more general language development of students. Lack of confidence in linguistic skills may result in students appearing more inarticulate or reticent in their contribution to lessons than is justified by their underlying understanding – for example, if asked to develop their ideas orally in front of their peers. All students are faced with problems of language, especially those with learning difficulties and those for whom English may not be their first language.

There are four interrelated problems, the first of which is the conceptual nature of the subject. Students need to be able to use terms such as 'democracy' or 'revolution' with confidence if they are to achieve higher levels of success in learning. This is compounded by history's lack of a specialised vocabulary. Teachers have to rely heavily on the everyday language students bring to class with them. As a result, ambiguity and confusion can arise over meanings associated with the simplest words and phrases. A Year 8 boy, when studying the English Civil War, asked: 'Is a civil war a war when people are nice to each other?' Added to this confusion is the fact that the everyday use of words may alter in their historical context. Sources for *Expansion, Trade and Industry* that contain the word 'factory' cannot be properly understood if students ascribe twentieth-century meanings to the word. This problem does not disappear as students progress from Year 7 through to Year 13. A level students are just as likely to ascribe modern meanings to words rather than consider meaning in its historical context. In recent tests with a mixed ability A level group of twenty students half gave the modern meaning of *'local authorities'* instead of the correct early nineteenth-century one.

The second difficulty relates to the high level of readability of materials for students. An examination of fifteen textbooks for Year 8 on the sixteenth and seventeenth centuries found that the average reading age was 12.7. This may be acceptable for brighter students but makes demands that are unrealistic as far as the less able are concerned. This situation is reproduced across the whole of secondary schooling. The difficulty is often not one of grammatical complexity but the density of ideas. History textbooks and worksheets contain a heavy concentration of information and concepts. Take, for example, a double page from the excellent *Discovering the Past Y9: Peace & War* on trying to get the vote, with a reading age, using the Fry Readability method, of 13.6. These are some of the concepts contained on pages 90–1: Whigs, Tories, landowners, revolution, democracy, Prime Minister, slide into a revolution, hardship, unemployment, electoral reform, demonstrations, reform organisations, Birmingham Political Union, general election, bill, act, MPs, bill passed by both Commons and Lords, majority, floodgates, adult men, contemporary, cartoon, counties, boroughs, occupying property, rotten boroughs, constituencies, contested, bribe, description, etc. Some are included in a glossary but most are not. This can create a formidable barrier to comprehension even in those passages that use the simplest syntax and choice of vocabulary. The message therefore is, by all means use textbooks but don't rely on them.

History involves much reading and the reading material used by departments must be chosen very carefully. In their management of resources heads of history need to develop a wide range of materials that students can use in class and outside. Reliance on a single textbook deprives students of the interest and excitement to be found in a variety of books or sources. Reading is not just a case of being able to comprehend what is written down. It also means being confident to use written materials through knowing how to use an index and the contents page to locate a particular piece of information.

Thirdly, there is the way that teachers use language in the classroom. Effective interaction between students and teachers, whether orally or in writing, means establishing a vocabulary that enables learning to occur and that students are happy with. Progression in student learning in history and their overall confidence and competence in using language will only be achieved if students understand the language used by their teachers, can sort out their own thoughts and communicate them successfully to others. History teachers need to consider this through student use of spoken language, reading and writing. A didactic approach to teaching is an important technique to employ in any history lesson, especially as a means of passing information to students. It can, however, end up as a passive process for students who listen to narratives, descriptions and explanations often without question or comment. Comprehension is shown later when the notes taken are written up. There is nothing like a well told story to motivate students at all levels in the secondary school but they need to become active participants in the learning process. Questioning, both closed and open, has an important part to play in this process. Planned discussions, debates, role-play and drama, carefully monitored, represent important opportunities for teachers to show students that their thoughts on history, even if wrong, are valued and provide an important way of developing interpretation and judgement.

Finally there is writing. It is the most common method of making historical statements especially as students move towards GCSE. It involves a range of skills (spelling, grammar, handwriting and presentation) and styles (note-taking, creative writing, essays, coursework, research assignments). History teachers have a major responsibility for helping students to write competently and with confidence. Healy (1994) argues that 'history itself is a type of composed work, a narrative which orders disparate occurrences into patterns of meaningful explanation'.

The use that students make of language varies. Some students are confident with talk and less so with writing and vice versa. History departments need to use the means of evaluation available to the English department in their assessment of student progression. If they are to manage the learning of students effectively then the uses made of language and the problems students encounter in this usage must form a major priority in teaching thinking.

Effective teaching and learning

The discussion above briefly sketches some of the elements that influence the extent to which students do or do not learn history. It is, however, important to recognise three different models that play a central role in effective learning (Brown, 1991a).

A *surface level of analysis* focuses on two crucial determinants of effective learning. The first is active learning time: the amount of time spent by students actively engaged in learning tasks designed to bring about planned educational outcomes. The second is quality of instruction. The quality of learning tasks and their appropriateness and suitability for bringing about the desired educational outcomes is central to this. Examining active learning time highlights time that is wasted in the classroom by both teachers and students. Observations of Year 7 and Year 10 mixed ability history classes suggest that this is as high as 30 per cent even with an experienced teacher. It is particularly relevant to student behaviour since disciplining individual students can disrupt the whole class. This model moves the focus of research away from a simple 'amount of time' notion towards exploring the nature of being 'actively engaged in the classroom'.

A *psychological level of analysis* extends the surface level of analysis by looking at the main features of student learning necessary for effective learning. Firstly, students must be attending to the learning experience. Secondly, students must be receptive to the learning experience. They must be motivated or, at least, be willing to learn from or respond to the experience. Finally, the learning experience must be appropriate for the desired learning to occur.

A *pedagogical level of analysis* is based, as far as possible, on the ways teachers think and talk about their own teaching. Teaching and learning are seen as managerial activities – the emphasis is on discipline (academic and behavioural), presentation and relationship with students. The role of expectations about learning by teachers and students is important and both have strategies for attempting to deal with and to meet the demands each makes on the other.

These three models raise a series of points relevant to all student learning in history on which teachers need to reflect:

- Have the desired outcomes of the learning experience in history been established clearly?
- In what ways will the learning experience ensure that active learning time is used to maximum effect? This raises the question of how behaviour is disciplined effectively in terms of time available.
- How appropriate is the learning task to the students? How are students with special needs catered for to enable them to achieve effective learning?
- What are the gender implications of the task?
- How do we ensure that students are attending to and are receptive of the learning experience?
- What expectations do we have of students individually and as a class?
- How is the learning experience managed from both the teaching and student viewpoints?

Figure 2.3 draws together the issues raised by these models for the history teacher. This leads the teacher on to the issue of student motivation. Learning history is, broadly, a combination of four things:

attention + storage of information + thinking + communication of information

For learning to be successful students have to be motivated in certain respects. Motivation is intrinsic or extrinsic. Intrinsic motivation involves an interest in the learning task for its own sake with satisfaction gained from its successful completion. Extrinsic or instrumental motivation sees a learning task as a means to an end. This may be contingent on the successful completion of the task but is not derived directly from the task itself. With extrinsic motivation the primary motives for learning appear to be attempts to earn status, esteem, acceptance and approval in the eyes of friends, peers, teachers and parents in both short- and long-term senses. This can be seen in students wanting to know how to move up the National Curriculum levels. The reverse of this is the avoidance of teacher reprimand and punishment. However, it needs to be recognised that some students appear to earn status by appearing not to learn, and are thus poorly motivated and disruptive.

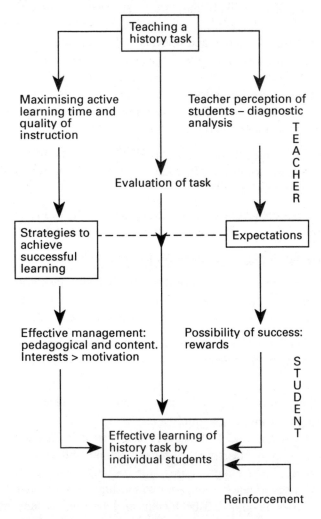

Figure 2.3 Models of analysis applied to history teaching

Achievement may be the most important feature of motivation. There are, however, two other dimensions that are important. Firstly, the maintenance of 'dignity' among students is crucial. The messages conveyed to students, often unintentionally, by teachers about values, attitudes and expectations act as a barrier to both motivation and achievement. Students maintain their sense of worth by opting out of tasks that have previously led to painful consequences: poor marks, teacher criticism, punishment or appearing 'dim' in front of peers. Secondly, learning tasks that require teachers or students to go beyond what is normally necessary can be seen as 'risky'. Risk occurs in students' perceptions of how likely they are to succeed in a particular task, the nature of the work itself, the nature of the mental effort and its apparent value in terms of interest and relevance. To motivate students in history the degree and especially the frequencies of risk need to be carefully controlled. Problem solving, for example, is a 'high risk' task whereas comprehension exercises form a 'low risk' enterprise. Figure 2.4 relates learning to motivation. This model raises a series of points that are relevant to all student learning experience in history:

- For most students motivation is extrinsic and the formal curriculum is a means to an end. In what ways does the history task enhance extrinsic motivation?

- How does teacher communication, either orally or in terms of written comments on work, enhance extrinsic motivation?

- How far does the learning task intend to enhance student esteem?

- How far does the design of the learning task – its clarity of purpose, level of interest, level of risk, degree to which it gives students control over their own learning – motivate learning?

- How far does the learning task give responsibility for managing learning to the student?

Students need to know where they are going in history. It removes uncertainty, aids learning autonomy and can enhance achievement. Managing learning is not simply a teacher responsibility.

Learning experiences are largely established by teachers. For those experiences to be effective they must maintain student attentiveness and receptiveness and be appropriate to the learning outcomes intended. This, along with sound teacher-student relationships, can do much to minimise student misbehaviour. Misbehaviour may be seen as any action by a student – overt or covert – which prevents that student, and others, from achieving the intended outcome of a learning experience. A distinction

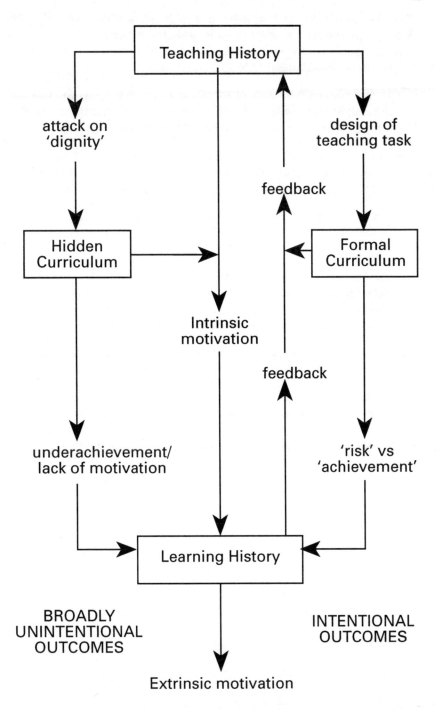

Figure 2.4 Model relating learning to motivation

must be made between actions that prevent learning and learning deficiencies, though the latter often leads to the former.

When assessing student misbehaviour in history lessons the following points can be considered:

- Is misbehaviour a result of the learning task? If so, is the task too difficult for the student or is the student having little success with it – failure or fear of failure as a cause of misbehaviour?

- Is the student bored with the task? Reacting to boredom by misbehaving is not restricted to low attainers but occurs across the ability range. Is extension material an appropriate response?

- Does the student suffer from specific learning difficulties? If so, how can the teacher mitigate them? How can teachers monitor them?

- What are the pay-offs for the students of misbehaving and how can the teacher counter them? The four most common pay-offs are attention seeking, causing excitement, malicious teasing and work avoidance. In each case the individual student is not learning effectively and there may be a knock-on effect on other students.

- Is the cause of the misbehaviour the result of social problems outside the direct influence of the school rather than a direct consequence of the learning situation in school?

Learning history is, as has been shown, a combination of coming to grips with what happened in the past and of developing conceptual and procedural understanding of that past. It is important that teachers recognise that though they frequently break learning down under convenient headings – 'Today's task focuses on chronology or causation' – learning is ultimately the ability of students to draw together these different elements to create a holistic understanding of the past.

CHAPTER 3

Assuring Quality

> Without change nothing is possible. Not to change is a sure sign of imminent extinction. Remember the dinosaurs! Whether change is comfortable or not, it is inevitable.
>
> Harvey Jones (1988, p.312)

Successful organisations anticipate and generate change because their survival depends on their ability to adapt and meet market needs. For schools change is problematic and they have traditionally been slow to adopt change mechanisms. Teachers are generally conservative in their attitudes and many resent having to make changes whether by agreement or compulsion. Parents are suspicious of change, which they often identify with non-traditional and progressive teaching and with a 'lowering of standards'. Students, like teachers, are conservative in their learning, adopting a low-risk approach in which didactic teaching is often more acceptable than active and experiential learning, not because it is more motivating but because, in their eyes, it ensures that the end product of good results is achieved. The wider public has a view of schooling often conditioned by its own experiences in school and by media coverage of the current situation. This bulwark of conservatism is and has long been a major reason why change has been pursued fitfully in schools.

This chapter explores the uneasy and sometimes uncertain relationship between learning and teaching in the history classroom. It considers the difficulties heads of history departments face in defining quality learning and the management issues they need to address. With Chapter 4 on team approaches to change and managing change, it suggests that collaborative management is the best way of assuring successful student learning of history.

The nature of quality

The ostrich is a strange creature, ungainly and in many respects a walking contradiction. Whether or not it sticks its head in the sand and hopes that dangers or threats will go away, it is assumed by many people to do so. Teachers, as reasonable and responsible individuals, you might think would not act like ostriches. You would, however, be wrong. To paraphrase, or perhaps parody, discussions in history departments across the country:

> Things are fine now, so let's not change!

> It won't work as far as my subject is concerned and I don't really want to change things anyway.

> My God! You can't possibly do this to history and anyway that's not what the government wants.

The first viewpoint can be called 'the ostrich position'. It is grounded in an uncritical view of experience using appeals to nostalgia. The second is the shrill clarion of emotion with the occasional reference to experience as a means of justification. The third is the reasoned, logical, analytical expression of departmental policy. It would be easy to dismiss the first argument as romantic retrospection; the second as essentially polemical and the third as representing vested interest with an unwillingness to take account of the broader picture. Most heads of history will find one or more of these views represented in their departments. However, each raises critical management problems and obstacles to achieving curriculum change and quality in learning history.

Learning history means looking to the future not the past

Teachers often feel uncomfortable with the notion of an educational market, especially those who look back to their teaching experiences. Notions of the curriculum as 'product', of 'clients', of 'selling' and of 'marketing' are perceived as ideas from an alien world. Education, most history teachers would argue, is valuable in its own right. Over two decades ago, when I started teaching, this may have been valid. Today it is far less so. Even then, for history teachers, the market played a key role when students were choosing their options post-14 and post-16. Why did some students opt for history while others did not? Teachers had to 'sell' their subject to compete effectively with other option subjects within the humanities and beyond. Students made choices on the basis of issues like the amounts of work involved and pass rates at O level, CSE and A level.

Though hidden, or at least not explicit, both teachers and students were aware of the potential market for the subject.

Today the language of the market is in practice central to teachers' decisions about learning. In simple terms the market for heads of history consists of their existing and potential clients. These include students and parents but they also embrace the broader community. Heads of history need to ask what the role of their subject is within the ever-changing agenda of academic, vocational and employment pathways. The history curriculum is a product that is 'sold' in the educational market. It is the service that history departments offer their clients. Three critical management questions arise from this (Brown, 1992a):

1. How far does the existing history curriculum reflect the composition of our clients and their identifiable needs?

2. If it does not, in what respects will changing that curriculum bring a closer correlation between clients and their needs and improved quality of learning?

3. How can a changed curriculum increase the market share of clients and in what ways?

Why do students 'buy' history?

The relationship between curriculums and clients is one of quality products and buyers. History departments, especially post-14, will not get clients unless their product is of sufficient quality. No department that wishes to be successful can neglect this simple economic fact. The history curriculum must empower departments within schools so that they can maximise student learning and product quality. To achieve this teachers need to be aware not just of the crucial interface between internal and external influences on quality learning but of what the relationship between the history curriculum and its clients actually is.

Whether clients 'buy' the history curriculum is, however, not simply a consequence of the product itself. There needs to be confidence in the quality of the curriculum within the client community and that is often the result of other factors. Take a situation where three teachers are responsible for Year 9 classes and when it comes to options the classes taught by two teachers largely opt for history while the third teacher's classes generally opt away from the subject. The 'perceptions' of students about teaching and learning and their 'image' of the subject play an important part in this context. How the subject is 'packaged' is similarly important. Students tend to opt for history teaching that is varied and

50

consequently motivating. Then there is the competition. A vibrant geography or religious studies department can lead to a fall in the numbers opting for history. Finally there are national directives that determine the framework, if not individual departmental teaching schemes, for history. In assessing the quality of learning in history it is essential that heads of department consider all these issues.

At Key Stage 3 there are guaranteed clients since the subject is mandatory. Post-14 this disappears and clients can always look elsewhere for their products. An analysis of why just over 600 Year 9 students in one school chose or did not choose history as an option for GCSE between 1991 and 1994 found that choice, irrespective of the ability of the students, was determined by

- The nature and especially the variety and clear structure of teaching.

- The interest shown by teachers in the students as individuals.

- The level of achievement of students, especially in Year 9 courses, measured in terms of their perceived success in the subject. For Year 9 students making their choice in 1994 reference was made in over 80 per cent of cases to movement up the National Curriculum Attainment Target levels.

- Consistent levels of success at GCSE in history.

The results of this survey were replicated for students choosing history as an A level subject. *What* students were taught mattered less than *how* they were taught.

Defining quality in learning history externally

You will know better than me the technical difficulty of measuring the movement of standards over time. Just as the basket of goods measured by the Retail Price Index is different from that many years ago, so the changing nature of subjects and syllabuses makes absolutely reliable comparisons of standards impossible.

Boswell (1994)

The nature of quality in learning history and of maintaining that quality is extremely difficult to define with precision. Take A level history for example. Successive Secretaries of State for Education have used the term 'gold standard' to suggest that A levels delineate the benchmark against which all other educational activities in history are evaluated and frequently found wanting. But is this the right way round? Heads of history need to ask deeper questions about their aims and values, about the nature of the quality of learning in their subject and by their students, about the diversity of student talent and about the different kinds of knowledge and skills worth learning in history (Pring, 1994). Quality in learning is part of a much broader canvas. It must be measured by outcomes but managers need to be clear about what outcomes they intend. Pigeon-holing students using external criteria alone does not mean that history departments have been successful in defining quality learning in history or of achieving that learning in their students at any more than a simple level.

Students and parents, however, do see learning in terms of success and failure. Because GCSE and A level and now National Curriculum Level Descriptions are regarded as *the* standards against which quality learning is judged students frequently label themselves by whether they have achieved GCSE grade C or A level grades A or B or Level Description 4 by the end of Year 9. This judgmental and in some cases hyper-critical attitude adopted by students and parents is understandable but it neither acknowledges the varieties of student ability nor reflects sufficiently their ability to learn effectively. All history teachers will have taught students who achieved GCSE grade C for whom that grade did not reflect quality learning or the real potential of the student and also those awarded grade F who have achieved far more than their ability suggested. Yet students, parents, and frequently teachers, would adjudge the first a success and the second a failure.

Teachers cannot escape this situation. Whether we admit it or not we all want highly motivated GCSE or A level students who will get good grades. Their results look good in league tables, enhance our self-esteem and status within our institutions, act as a catalyst for procuring high quality students in the future through result-oriented option systems, and enable us to sustain our market share in the whole-school curriculum against competition from other subjects. The problem with defining quality in terms of the objective standards of external criteria is that it usually results in approaches to teaching and learning that do not take account of the individual character and needs of students. Yet 'products' in a general sense *are* judged in the market context. A computer that does not give efficient service will not sell. The dilemma for individual teachers and heads of history is that they need to define quality learning both in terms of the needs and abilities of individual students and of objective external standards. Managers of history need to recognise clearly that quality in learning cannot be defined on the basis of a single criterion. The aim for teachers of history should be to encourage and develop their students to demonstrate their learning effectively under what are, in the context of their total learning, atypical situations. Yet they must also recognise that the quantitative performance of students in examinations, at any level from Year 7 to Year 13, is a necessary but not sufficient criterion of quality in learning. Figure 3.1 attempts to portray the teachers' dilemma.

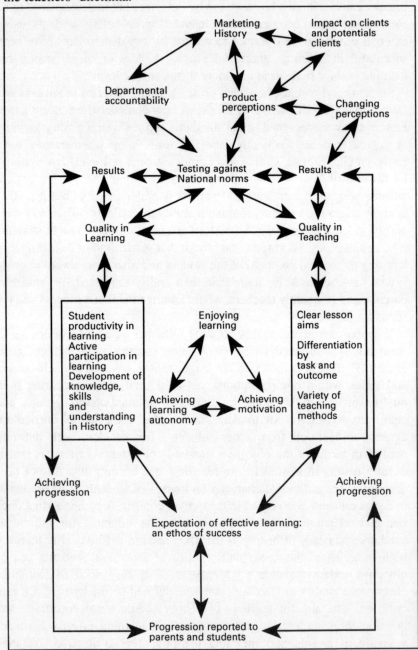

Figure 3.1 Criteria and goals in history teaching

Improving quality in learning history

Improving the quality of student learning is a collaborative process. It involves teachers and students within schools and parental support outside. It is about establishing good teaching and learning relationships and having confidence that learning can be successful irrespective of the ability and initial motivation of students. It is about development and accountability for both teachers and students. But it is an uncertain process (Murgatroyd and Morgan, 1993). The difficulty history teachers face is that they cannot be quite sure that what is being taught is what their planning intended or that there is a guaranteed way of teaching to enable students to learn. An identical lesson plan on medieval castles was used with two mixed ability groups in Year 7 but with very different outcomes. Both groups were tested two days after the lessons. In one group twenty-three students had achieved Attainment Target 3 level 3 or 4 while in the other only twelve had achieved these levels. The teacher was asked why she thought this was the case but she had no answer other than that one lesson was in the morning and the other after lunch. This may well have had a bearing on student learning but it does not explain why the following week the first group achieved lower levels of achievement in AT3 than the second group. Teachers have to work with this uncertainty in student learning and no pat answers or alleged conclusive proof can resolve totally this continuing dilemma.

Learning history cannot be reduced to a series of elements of knowledge and skill. It depends on the development of a complex weave of interrelated objectives and components that interact with students who are not empty vessels to be filled or moulded in the image of their teachers. This complex interaction of the history curriculum with students and their different motivations and capacities to learn has to be managed effectively by teachers if quality learning is to occur, to be maintained and developed. Effective learning requires collaborative interaction with students so that the designed learning environment facilitates student progression. This is a process of creative construction of student learning experience and requires continuous reflection by teachers on their teaching and on their students' progress (see Majaro, 1988). Quality teaching and learning are continuously creative activities (Goddard and Leask, 1992).

In simple terms, teachers identify objectives of teaching, teach the lesson, evaluate learning and, having reflected on this, modify their intended outcomes for the next time they teach a topic.

Figure 3.2 illustrates the process.

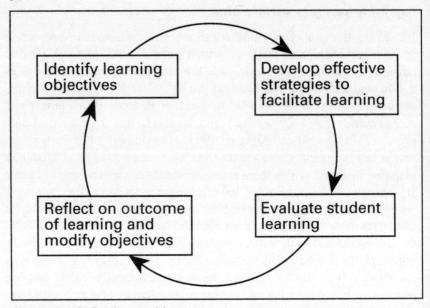

Figure 3.2 Reflective teaching

Heads of department, with their teaching staff, will identify the learning objectives to be achieved through particular lessons. These will find their way into the departmental scheme of work. This policy document signals direction. It should provide a clear and agreed statement of the values, vision and principles that underpin the history curriculum. This statement is crucial if every teacher in the department is to understand the curriculum framework but it will not tell individual teachers how to deliver lessons to their own classes. A history curriculum could be produced as a step-by-step instruction manual but it would stifle the creativity of teachers and significantly restrict the extent that students could learn. Teachers must have the flexibility to respond to the particular learning needs of students. However, the curriculum policy, developed with the full involvement of teachers in departments, must inform fully the teaching and learning process. This is a creative process where learning quality is dependent on a full understanding of what has to be done, coupled with a considerable degree of professional commitment to the adaptation process by teachers in history departments.

Managing by objectives almost without exception focuses on maintaining learning practices rather than transforming them to achieve progressive learning quality. It adopts what has been called a 'do what we always do but do it slightly better' strategy and, as a consequence, is rarely successful in achieving radical changes in the learning abilities of students. Schaffer (1991) argues that the inability to use management by objectives to achieve quality performance is due to two 'habits'. Firstly, managers believe that past practice is able to meet future needs. The focus is on the history teacher determining both the nature of teaching and the learning strategies students need to develop to achieve the teacher-determined objectives. There is no real collaboration between teacher and student in the learning process. Secondly, managers rely on procedures to solve learning problems rather than changing the learning process itself. Both these habits are endemic in schools but they may well lead heads of history to 'attack performance problems from the wrong angle in the wrong place with the wrong people at the wrong time' (Murgatroyd and Morgan, 1993, p.133). Quality learning in history may well be about students knowing which procedures result in which outcomes but, at its heart, learning history is a process that has to be addressed successfully if it is to be of quality.

Management by objectives is certainly a safe way of achieving modest levels of improved learning. Heads of history, however, may wish to pursue the setting and development of 'outrageous' goals. These are technically referred to as 'Hoshin goals' and are goals that challenge teachers and students to go beyond what they currently think themselves capable of achieving. Hoshin planning is grounded in the following principles:

- *Participation*. All history teachers should be involved in the application of the school's mission statements to the department. Heads of history provide leadership to achieve this end.

- *Empowerment*. Individual teachers must be allowed the power and responsibility to introduce learning initiatives within this overall framework.

- *Attack causes*. The root causes, rather than the symptoms, of students' inability to learn effectively are tackled directly.

- *Take risks*. Constant improvement involves taking risks. Peters (1989) suggests that 'if you don't fail some of the time, you're not trying'.

- *The Key is Quality.*

- *Communicate, communicate and then communicate some more.* Heads of history need to communicate their pedagogical vision to their teams. Teachers need to communicate with each other about their work, successes, failures, methods and ideas. Students need to communicate their hopes, opportunities, failures, successes and ideas through action planning. Communication is the lynch-pin of effective quality learning. It is about teachers walking around and discussing learning with students.

- *Focus on process*. Effective outcomes follow effective processes. Students need to ask, as much as teachers, 'What is preventing me from and helping me to develop the process of learning history?'

These principles challenge individual students to go beyond what they think themselves capable of achieving. They are grounded in expecting students to achieve higher levels of learning than they believe possible. The following process can be used as a basis for putting these principles into practice:

1. Students are encouraged to identify their learning difficulties in history through action planning. They are asked to address the following questions:

   - *What errors do I make in my work?* These may be either substantive historical errors, for example, a problem with identifying the causes of a particular event, or more general learning difficulties like problems with spelling or expression in writing.

   - *How can I make fewer errors in my work?* Students are here asked to identify how they feel they can make significant improvements in the quality of their learning and the role they feel their teachers can play in this.

   - *How can I maximise the use of my time in class and for homework?* Students are being asked to recognise that learning is not simply about the amount of time they spend on something but that quality learning requires that time is used effectively. It is actual learning time not time itself that is the issue.

In essence, students are being asked to identify those areas that they feel prevent them from achieving quality learning in history, how they think they can overcome these problems and how their teachers can help.

2. Teachers then need to consider student responses, looking very carefully at what has been written. Three particular things need to be looked for:

   - The ideas that students have for what they would do to improve their quality of learning.

   - The barriers that they feel prevent them from putting improvements into effect.

- The degree to which they are committed to implementing improvements to the quality of their learning.

This needs to be followed up by teachers discussing student responses individually or, if there is a general problem, collectively to clarify points of uncertainty and to check their understanding of student perceptions of problems.

3. Identifying outrageous goals involves two parallel processes. Individual students need to identify what their individual goals should be. The timescale for achieving these goals will depend on the age, motivation and ability of students. Year 7 students respond better to short-term goals while A level students are capable of sustaining goals over a longer timescale. Teachers may also wish to identify whole-class goals, arguably within the context of National Targets, to be achieved by the year 2000 relating, for example, to the percentage of students who should achieve GCSE grades A-C or the contribution history can make to stay-on rates post-16. The goals should challenge everyone but they must be goals that everyone can see the value of achieving.

4. Empower every individual in the class to achieve these goals. It needs to be made clear that the goals represent the most significant challenges for the future of the individual students. Once agreed, the WHATs are non-negotiable but the HOWs are a matter for individual students. This gives students the power to determine how they can achieve their own goals: they are free to experiment, risk and develop new ways of working provided that they can be seen to be working towards the goals that they have agreed. The history teacher's role is to provide support, give direction where necessary and celebrate success and learn from failure as progress is made.

5. Progress needs to be monitored constantly. Students should be required to show what they are doing towards achieving their goals. Teachers should maximise and share comments, both good and bad, and in doing so make student commitment tangible and real.

The purpose of Hoshin planning is to focus individual and class energies through the creation of challenging goals to which students feel that they can be committed. Higher levels of learning can be achieved through the setting of challenging goals for which students will have a strong sense of personal ownership than through conventional management by objective techniques.

So does Hoshin planning result in improved quality learning in history? Two groups of students were monitored using this technique between

1992 and 1994. The first group consisted of forty-eight GCSE students taught in two mixed ability classes. All were asked at monthly intervals during the course to identify goals they wished to achieve and were given considerable flexibility as to how they could achieve those goals. Where agreed goals were not met students had to justify their failure before identifying goals for the following month. In some cases failure was due to an unrealistic goal but, interestingly, even where failure occurred for this reason, under most circumstances considerable strides towards its achievement had been made. Students were asked each term to assess how they thought the course was developing. Three types of comment were frequently made:

- 'I'm using my time more effectively'. 'It allows me to plan my time better than before'. 'I didn't realise how much time I wasted in class before.'

- 'I'm much clearer about what I'm learning and how to do it properly.' 'I'm doing better, I can remember more that I've done in class and at home.' 'I didn't know how to learn before, now I do and it makes me feel good.'

- 'I feel I have some control over how I learn and I know that if it goes wrong then I can talk to my teacher about it.' 'I feel I want to learn, I didn't think that way before.' 'Knowing you've achieved something gives you a real buzz!'

So the students felt that they had achieved more but was this the case? Viewed objectively in terms of marks assessed for the examination there is ample evidence to demonstrate that a higher quality of learning was occurring. Coursework marks, a good indicator of student commitment and planning, were, across all student abilities, an average 18 per cent higher than in previous years when Hoshin planning had not been used. A similar situation was evident with GCSE results. Viewed subjectively, levels of motivation were higher, commitment to serious and productive work was almost universal, homework was invariably handed in on time and where it was not students did not hide from the teacher but volunteered why before the lesson. Levels of detention were low – only three students in two years – and levels of commendation were high, with all students at one stage of the course receiving commendation awards and most students on more than one occasion.

The second group consisted of thirty Year 9 top set students. The National Curriculum history levels from the middle schools showed that most students were on Level 3 with six on Level 4 and one on Level 5. This provided a clear base on which to build. Experience with Year 9 students suggests that they often arrive at upper schools with a preconceived view of history and know that they can opt out of the subject at the end of the year. Motivating students by involving them in identifying learning needs and goals to achieve more effective learning was therefore a priority from the outset. Careful lesson planning with the use of a variety of teaching methods proved effective in achieving motivation and interest. Focusing work on particular attainment targets with written and verbal comments to students – the notion of communicating and communicating some more – provided an important stimulus to progressive and effective learning. Student assessments of their progress on a monthly basis with goals for the next month agreed and with plans for implementing them helped all students to move through the different levels. By the end of the course all students had added at least two levels overall to their middle school scores and a third of students had achieved or were heading towards Level 7. In their final assessment of the course they were asked to evaluate in what ways their learning had improved and why. The responses proved similar to those for the GCSE groups. One notable consequence of this approach to quality learning was that 75 per cent of the students opted for history for Years 10 and 11. For a parallel control group only 35 per cent of students opted for history. Not only can effective process planning enable students to improve the quality of their learning but it can enhance the ways students perceive the subject within the competitive market of the option system.

Improving the quality of learning history requires students to develop effective strategies for pinpointing their own weaknesses, for developing strategies through the process of identifying attainable goals in collaboration with their teachers and for monitoring and evaluating learning performance against those goals. Effective learning is a partnership between students with the confidence that they can produce work of assured quality and a sense of 'feeling comfortable' with work in the classroom and outside and teacher expectation that students can be successful.

History teaching and assuring quality in learning

In schools, teachers are supposed to help students participate in the 'community of subject matter', whose objective content of thought and experience – systems, theories and ideas – are impersonal because they are distinct from the people who learn or discuss them.

Buchmann (1993, p.147)

Teaching history, like learning history, is an intensely personal thing. It involves the sometimes tense relationship between respect for knowledge and for students. It is not detached. Teachers have two main tasks: to stretch the students' world by presenting an effective selection of the past worlds with which they are in contact and to work collaboratively with students in their struggle towards knowledge and understanding of those worlds (Noddings, 1984). Yet to assist and contribute to student learning entails unending puzzles and uncertainties. History teachers cannot be sure, any more than any teacher can be sure, how a lesson will go or exactly what students will learn (Jackson, 1986). The second part of this chapter considers what we mean by effective history teaching and how this affects quality student learning.

Teaching certainties and uncertainties and learning history

Marland (1975, p.100) argues persuasively that there is a 'craft' of the classroom: 'The more "organised" you are, the more sympathetic you can be. The better your classroom management, the more help you can be to your pupils.' He is, of course, right. Students need and like routines and teachers need them to respond to the variety of situations they face. Research evidence (for example, Brown and McIntyre, 1993) shows that students see good teachers as being those who do not have problems with control and are organised. Certainty in the classroom has many advantages for teachers and students (Floden and Buchmann, 1993). Being able to predict the results of actions accurately allows teachers to choose the most effective strategies for achieving their desired outcomes. Being certain about the effects of different teaching approaches lets teachers select instructional approaches based on their probable impact on student learning. Certainty helps them avoid confrontations and heavy-handed actions that suppress students' sense of personal responsibility and maintains their dignity. History teachers who favour certainty may choose content that can be tested by traditional objective questions rather than making decisions on the basis of what is worthwhile for students to learn. Certainty gives teachers control. This can lead to rigidity and narrowness in the classroom rather than flexibility, breadth and outrageous goals and to the mistaken sense that for teaching to be successful it needs to be mechanical.

This suggests that teaching and learning are more concerned with history as a subject and with transmitting the content and context of history – more predictable and static, that is, than they are in practice. This contrasts sharply with the research evidence collected through detailed observation of classrooms. Doyle (1986) draws attention to six major features of teaching:

1. It is *multidimensional*: many activities go on in a busy history lesson and effective learning is affected by the varying learning and other agendas of students. This means that teachers have to make choices almost continually and these are rarely simple. Year 8 students have been engaged on group assignments on the Civil War for three weeks. Some think they have finished. Others are still battling with the issue. What choices should the teacher make? Should she stop work and move on to something else or risk continuing for another week to allow all to finish? There are costs and benefits associated with this choice: loss of motivation for those who have, in their words, 'done'; frustration for those who still have work to do.

2. It has *simultaneity*: teachers are involved in many tasks at the same time.

3. It has *immediacy*: these tasks have an immediacy that demands response or intervention with little or no advanced notice.

4. It is *unpredictable*: research may offer illuminating pointers to the overall merits of different teaching approaches. It does not, and probably never will, permit accurate predictions of what *this* student will learn from *this* lesson taught in *this* way in *this* school. It is difficult to explain why a student can understand the causes of the Reformation one lesson but appear to have lost that understanding by the next lesson.

5. It is *public*: both teachers and students are on view in a public forum in which interaction and collaboration cannot be taken for granted and where disciplining one student may have unforeseen consequences on the rest of the class.

6. It has *its own history*: this is a consequence of weeks of interaction between teacher and students resulting in each class having its own way of working and its own expectations. This dynamism of the classroom is at the heart of effective student learning in history.

Teachers are uncertain about many things: about teaching, how and what students learn, predicting how students will act and react and about their authority in the classroom. Appreciating this can be unsettling, leading to pedagogical confusion and loss of confidence. Too much uncertainty may be disabling for both teachers and students. Yet it is the essential driving force behind successful history teaching. Take a Year 7 class on the Battle of Hastings. The story of what happened that fateful day on the slopes of Senlac Hill is to the fore. The class is enthralled by the sequence of events. The Saxon forces lined up on the hill, the Normans below them. The attacks, the feints, the arrows and the terror and anarchy of the final Saxon collapse. The impact of the story – and this is where I would prefer to see teaching history as an art rather than a craft – lies in the interweaving of the expected and the surprising. The teacher may have planned the learning outcomes of the lesson carefully but it is the pertinent, or sometimes impertinent, questions from students that provide unexpected opportunities for teaching and learning. This is clearly reflected in many OFSTED reports on history. Nothing is better designed to stifle student creativity and motivation than teachers rooting out uncertainties wherever they find them. Balancing openness and predictability is difficult and dependent on context but it is crucial to teaching and the learning of students and teachers alike. Good history teaching, like good history, should thrive on uncertainty.

Teacher knowledge and learning history

Teachers' knowledge of their professional roles plays a central part in determining the effectiveness of student learning. This knowledge has several dimensions. Stanford University's 'Teacher Assessment Project' and 'Knowledge Growth in a Profession Project' studied inexperienced and experienced history teachers (Shulman, 1986; Wilson, Shulman and Rickert, 1987). These researchers found that the 'pedagogical content knowledge' of history was only one aspect of teachers' professional knowledge but the Stanford project found it to be a crucial ingredient in teacher performance particularly in their fluency and confidence in the classroom. Pedagogical content knowledge is the distinctive kind of knowledge that teachers need to transform their knowledge of the content of history into something interesting and comprehensible to students. Shulman has been primarily concerned to draw attention to this as an essential part of the work that teachers are employed to do. Experienced teachers have a large repository of content knowledge on which they can draw in the classroom that inexperienced teachers do not have. They also have a 'vision of history', a perception of the subject 'as a human construction, an enterprise in which people try to solve a puzzle.' Specialist but inexperienced history teachers tend to have a similar perception of the subject to their more experienced colleagues. They are more sensitive to the importance of interpretation, to the multi-dimensional nature of causation and to the significance of a broader contextual approach to the subject. Non-specialists appear not to become better history teachers simply by accumulating a larger store of content knowledge, largely because their conceptions of history remain naïve and distorted. The National Curriculum makes content demands on teachers in areas where they often do not have the necessary expertise. This raises important management questions for departments consisting largely of non-specialists and the research suggests that this may affect the ability of students, especially those in Years 7 to 9 where non-specialists are more frequently used, to learn the subject effectively. The conclusions of the Stanford project are backed up by several other studies: Burke (1987); Smyth (1987, pp.19–34, 45–54); Calderhead (1988, 1994); Day (1990, 1993).

Eraut (1988) suggests that a typology of *management knowledge* can be used as a means of developing the professional abilities of teachers. Though designed as a management tool, its six categories provide a useful framework for history teachers to consider their existing pedagogy, to think about their experiential knowledge and how it might best be further developed and applied to developing quality student learning. Eraut's six categories are *knowledge of people, situation knowledge, knowledge of educational practice, conceptual knowledge, process knowledge* and *control knowledge*.

Managing student learning is strongly influenced by knowledge of the students involved and by knowledge of how other teachers deal with learning situations. This is often acquired unintentionally through interactions that have other purposes. Teacher knowledge is likely to be changed by seeing students in different contexts and situations. The impact this has on developing learning goals is threefold:

1. It focuses teacher attention on the impact that their behaviour has on students and on their assumptions about students.

2. The more knowledge that teachers have of students, the more reliable and reflective the manner in which their learning can be developed.

3. The development of knowledge of people allows teachers to develop a more rounded view of students and allows them to change their minds about student learning potential.

Heads of history need to ensure that their departments have as much information about student learning as possible. This is essential at transition from one school to another, a powerful argument for effective liaison as one of their major roles.

Situational knowledge consists of many types of information related to different features of the teaching and learning situation in the classroom. Decision-making that enables effective learning to occur demands that teachers have as much information as possible. This knowledge is constructed partly through discussion with students and reflection on their statements, but there is also much intuitive assumption. New information and new perspectives will result in situational knowledge changing as teachers become more aware of their own assumptions and the learning needs of their students.

Knowledge of educational practice is acquired consciously and deliberately by teachers. For history teachers this covers many aspects of education and schooling from classroom practice to external relations and marketing. Within departments no one person can be expected to be knowledgeable in every area of educational practice and one of the important management skills heads of history must develop is the ability to use the expertise of all members of their departments to the full. This pedagogical dimension is paralleled by conceptual knowledge or what can be called knowledge of subject. Effective learning, as we have already seen, requires history teachers to have assimilated the values, principles, ideas, theories, methodologies and knowledge of the subject. The problem is the transfer of learning between academic, whole-school discussion and classroom action contexts. Process knowledge provides the means for getting things done and establishes a linkage between knowledge of educational practice and conceptual knowledge. Control knowledge is the final dimension of management knowledge. It includes self-awareness and sensitivity about one's strengths and weaknesses, the need for self-management, prioritisation and delegation and the skills one uses in organising and controlling one's thinking. This applies to both students and teachers.

The notion of the 'reflective practitioner', developed by Schon (1983, 1987), is useful in drawing together the discussion on teaching. It is an attractive idea since it helps history teachers to consider, analyse, evaluate and, as a result, change their own practice (Rudduck, 1988). It heightens their awareness of the contexts in which they work and empowers them to take greater control over their own professional development. It enables teachers to consider the complexities of the teaching and learning processes and their predictability and uncertainties. Observation of colleagues' lessons, with feedback sessions in which the quality of student learning is discussed, has proved a highly successful form of 'reflection-in-action'.

Professional understanding and assuring quality

Teaching is a complex process and the precise relationship between good teaching and quality learning is difficult to establish. It is, however, possible to draw certain conclusions that will help history teachers make sense of their teaching. Firstly, there are elements of teaching that are predictable and for which learning is helped if effective and agreed learning and procedural routines are established in the classroom. Secondly, there is a clear link between the professional knowledge of teachers and the ability of students to learn effectively. Thirdly, teachers can improve their ability to help students to learn by reflecting on their current practice and, when necessary, changing it. Finally, student learning is enhanced by the communicative skills of teachers.

Making sense of teaching and learning or managing history as a performing art

Vaill (1989) suggests that the metaphor of 'management as a performing art' is a useful point of departure for managers to explore the challenges that confront them in the modern organisation. I want to use this notion as a way of making sense of the discussion of teaching and learning history. Vaill identifies the notion of 'permanent white water' as the conditions of permanent turbulence and unpredictability under which managers operate. This means that merely adjusting or fine tuning our understanding of the management role is no longer sufficient to deal with the management problems that face us. In teaching and learning history it is possible to argue that the events of the last decade, the various National Curriculums, the debate on what history should be taught and how it should be assessed, reflect this notion of 'white water'. The point of Vaill's conceptual analysis of management and why it is important to history teachers is that it allows them to focus their attentions not simply on a functional model of management in which routines and procedures dominate but on teaching and learning as interwoven creative processes. Hoshin planning takes teachers away from the mechanistic method of management by objectives towards a process of teaching and learning in which history teachers are not just concerned with *what* students learn but *how* they can learn more effectively.

Teaching history as a performing art picks up the dynamic and fluid quality of the classroom experience. The primary objective of a performance in, say, drama or ballet is achieving a rounded performance as a whole. It is the whole rather than the component parts that is important. For history teachers it allows a focus on the whole process of learning history rather than, as we so often do, breaking it down into its component parts. There is no danger that teachers will then confuse student proficiency in one component, such as understanding of causation or chronology, with their overall proficiency in the subject as a whole. Thinking of student learning as a performing art encourages consideration of both the whole and the parts in relation to each other. It also allows a more realistic consideration of what a *quality* performance is. There is nothing automatic or formulaic about it, no canned definition of quality that can be taken off the shelf. What we have to do when evaluating quality learning in history is a complex integration between what we want and feel that students can achieve in their particular situations with what are perceived as being the more timeless, more objective standards of quality and of taste. This is a far more creative process than the often one-dimensional, though necessary, departmental discussions of whether students have completed a particular module of work. If managing student learning is a performing art, then the consciousness and reflectiveness of teachers are transformed. They become increasingly interested in the quality of the process and much more aware of how a given course of action does or does not lead to effective learning. Teachers are *thinking* of quality throughout.

The notion of quality teaching and learning as a process deserves further thought. Do we achieve quality learning if students reach their particular goals by whatever means possible? Do the means justify the ends? If high levels of learning history are found to be achieved by teachers dictating notes to silent students are we justified in saying that students are achieving quality learning? I think not. The performing arts would hold themselves to staying within certain forms in pursuit of the intended results. If the forms are violated, the result is not of the same value. There is more to successful learning that simply achieving quality performances. In fact quality cannot be achieved in any real sense without involving students in the pleasure of the past. Personal enjoyment by students, as the performing arts show unequivocally, does not detract from getting the job done and almost certainly enables the job to be done better. Students who take pleasure in learning history and are consequently motivated by it are more likely to produce quality learning.

Vaill identifies three further qualities in any organised activity that the performing arts unmistakably demonstrate: 'particularity', 'variety' and 'contextuality'. By particularity Vaill (1989, p.120) means 'the utter uniqueness and concreteness of every event.' The performing arts seek magic in each performance and that is what needs to be sought in student learning. Each student will learn in his or her own way. Their learning is unique and should not be put in the strait-jacket of routine. Quality learning in history should celebrate the uniqueness of student learning with its successes and inevitable failures. Then, variety and the move towards unity. Students within a class react to the same situations differently and it takes time to achieve an organic feeling of unity within a class towards both the teacher and the subject. Participants in a play do not immediately have a feeling of unity any more than a class of Year 7 history students. Lastly, contextuality or in slang terms 'chemistry'. Why do some students look forward to their history lessons while others have a sense of foreboding when the lesson bell goes and exhilaration afterwards? How does this affect student ability to learn? The contextual link between teacher and learner is crucial. The performing arts show that people can learn to integrate their consciousness as well as their actions. They can come to share a common vision and common standards while leaving room for their own individuality. Effective learning is not possible without integration at this level. Without this learning can become a stilted and tentative performance that lacks rhythm and flow. This creative dimension enriches learning. The performing arts reveal the individual's potential for generating new interpretations and perceptions, things that go far beyond what previously seemed possible. The same applies to learning history. An ethos of quality in the classroom – the belief by teachers that students can achieve higher levels of learning in history and the recognition that this can only be achieved through a sympathetic and symbiotic relationship between teacher and student in which both are learners in different ways – is at the heart of achieving and assuring quality in the history classroom.

CHAPTER 4

Changing History Collaboratively

'Change forces' is a deliberate *double entendre*. Change is ubiquitous and relentless, forcing itself on us at every turn. At the same time, the secret of growth and development is learning how to contend with the forces of change – turning positive forces to our advantage, while blunting negative ones. The future of the world is a learning future.

Fullan (1993, p.vii)

Improving the quality of student learning in history is about successfully achieving change in people. People, not structures, are the agents of growth and change. Innovation is always uncertain and often painful, a journey to an unknown destination, a problem for teachers and students for whom certainty is generally more acceptable than uncertainty. This is nothing new. The idea of the learning individual and institution has been around for three decades (Garratt, 1987). What is new is a growing understanding of how change and people interact, of the tensions that are created and how they may be resolved, of the breakthroughs and failures, and of the insights history teachers can gain from addressing the issue of change and its impact on student ability to learn effectively. The key is to be the agent rather than the victim of change. This chapter suggests that if we are to enable students to learn history effectively then as individual teachers and departments we have to address the issues of change from a radical perspective. Tinkering with what we have is no longer enough. Prescription will not do. I intend to do this by considering four issues: notions of leadership and collegiality, the nature of change, teachers and the history department, how managing the learning of history collaboratively by teams of teachers is the only effective way forward and, finally, how to make change stick.

Leadership and collegiality

Collegiality and leadership are central to the success of history departments in achieving quality student learning. The nature of these management ideas has changed in recent years. Leadership is no longer seen in terms of the manipulations and prescriptive strategic planning of heads of history. Collegiality is about ownership and personal vision-building rather than a contrived process for achieving structural change.

Leadership and collaboration

Marland (1971) was the first writer to encourage heads of department to understand their roles. He identified the pivotal nature of the role – something reiterated in the NFER research (Earley and Fletcher-Campbell, 1989) – and stressed the importance of delegation and communication so that a 'complementary team' might be fostered in a 'climate of discussion'. Before Marland wrote, the role of the head of history was largely unproblematic, curriculum and pedagogy were traditional, relatively static and largely unquestioned. It had evolved largely in grammar schools and, following the reorganisation of secondary schools along comprehensive lines, needed to be modified, especially with the development of the notion of 'middle management'. The result was a shift from the head of history perceived as an acknowledged expert on history to a far broader, multifaceted role in which expertise in the content of history *per se* held a decreasingly significant place. Heads of history became team-leaders, skilled in the management of change, and staff developers to ensure the effectiveness of their departmental teams.

There is a major problem for anyone writing about the role of the head of department. One would have expected that there would be a significant degree of similarity and consensus in the way departments operate. It is clear, however, that this is far from being the case (see, for example, research on twenty-four comprehensive schools, Torrington and Weightman, 1989, pp.162–72). Marland (1981, p.2) starts with a list of duties of the head of department – what may broadly be called a 'prescriptive approach' – and this has been echoed in Higham (1979) and Clare (1989) for the role of the head of history. This approach seems to have become the current orthodoxy among headteachers and advisers and it is common to find such lists in school and departmental handbooks. Prescriptions are useful as an indication of what heads of history ought to be doing but they can be so utopian that they correspond little to what heads of history do in practice. A prescriptive style imposes order, allows for a lot of co-ordination with little duplication of effort and allows resources to be allocated across history departments on a rational basis. It is most appropriate for dealing with matters that are predictable and routine. The focus is on procedures and systems, upon what many head teachers call 'good management'. The result, however, is that heads of history can end up ticking off lists of duties and supervising and monitoring the work of their departmental staff rather than engaging creatively and dynamically with their central pedagogical and managerial imperative of improving the quality of student learning.

This is not to deny the importance of routine administrative or structural tasks. Heads of history would rightly be criticised if, for example, they failed to enter students for examinations or did not respond to notes from senior management. Neither can they abdicate their responsibility for monitoring and judging the performance of their staff. The successful head of department does all these things but within a framework of 'leadership styles'. These do not lend themselves to the sort of comforting specificity favoured by prescriptive literature. There is, however, a growing body of research that suggests the pre-eminence of leadership over prescriptive duties: for example, Bennis and Nanus (1985) and Peters and Austin (1994). Rutter *et al.* (1979) found that end products were more favourable in schools where there was a combination of leadership and a decision-making process in which all teachers felt their views were being represented. Effective leadership by heads of history is about managing the people in their departments, whether students or other teachers, rather than simply making sure that procedures are followed. The roles of heads of history, in this context, are facilitative and developmental rather than instructional or controlling. Their status in the organisation hierarchy, whether departmental or whole-school, comes less from their length of service than from their ability to lead their teams through issues or concerns or activities. This approach can promote a sense of purpose and vision and staff often feel valued personally in this situation. It, tends, however, to be *the leader's* vision and *the leader's* purpose so there is a strong element of control in the leadership style. In certain circumstances this may be beneficial to history departments. In periods of stability leaders can make control more acceptable by communicating their vision and by humanising procedures. In periods of crisis, like poor examination results, a strong leader can embody what needs to be done and so help the department in creating a new purpose. There is collaboration within departments here but it is generally 'contrived'. One problem is that 'following the leader' can be frustrating and inhibiting for staff who cannot develop their own personal visions without threatening the leader. This reduces flexibility and uncertainty, both of which are essential if effective change in student learning is to be achieved. Effective leadership comes out of an effective cultural context rather than the other way round. As Hargreaves (1994) shows clearly it is through 'collaborative or collegial' rather than contrived cultures that effective change occurs. The focus is not upon procedures or control but on collectives processes. It allows individual teachers to participate in their own voices in departmental management.

The effective running of history departments is rarely the result of just one of these three managerial styles. There are occasions where prescription may be appropriate especially when consistency is important as, for example, with departmental policies for marking students' work. Leadership can be helpful where there is uncertainty that needs to be dealt with quickly. Collaborative cultures are essential where the full and voluntary commitment of all history teachers is necessary. Torrington and Weightman (1989) concluded from their research that 'the ideal of almost all our 1,065 respondents and hundreds of other people we have spoken with in discussing our findings, is the Leadership style...' Though they added, 'we find this severely limited for most of the situations which schools now face, and all too often teachers themselves – especially those in senior posts – perpetuate this dangerous dependence on one person.' Collaborative cultures may not be as comfortable for heads of history and they certainly provide them with less control. However, if they are to realise their prime imperative of achieving effective student learning such cultures provide the only effective approach to managing history in changing times.

A Culture of collaboration

Collaboration can be seen as constituting 'the metaparadigm of educational and organisational change in the postmodern age...as articulating and integrating principles of action, culture, development, organization and research'. (Hargreaves, 1994, pp.244–5) There is significant research evidence showing that collaboration fosters teacher development, forms a vital part of school improvement and leads to increasing departmental and school effectiveness. We do, however, need to be clear what we *mean* by collaboration and collegiality if history departments are to be able to develop them as the central planks for achieving change in student learning.

It is important for heads of history to recognise two things. Firstly, collaboration is *not* an absolute. As Hargreaves (1994, p.188) says, 'there is no such thing as "real" or "true" collaboration or collegiality'. Collaboration takes different forms and serves different purposes. A history department may claim to adopt a collaborative approach to designing new modules of work but embrace joint work in the classroom only on rare occasions. Heads of history need to take time to decide what they and their departments understand its meaning to be for them.

Secondly, Hargreaves (1994, p.188) argues that this leads 'inexorably to questions about who guides and controls collaboration and collegiality; about their micropolitics.' Has collaboration between members of a history department emerged as a consequence of debate within the department or has the head of department or the senior management decided that it would be a 'good thing to do'? The first implies some sort of shared culture by members of a department, the latter a top-down decision motivated by considerations like administrative control. Hargreaves argues that there is a 'pivotal' difference between a 'collaborative culture' and an administratively constructed or 'contrived collegiality'.

Contrived collegiality is a structural solution to collaboration and is a common feature of history departments. It is, according to Hargreaves (1994, pp.195–6), administratively regulated, compulsory, implementation-oriented, fixed in time and space and predictable. The head of history decides that he wants to introduce a new system of reporting, believing that this would act as an important stimulus to student achievement. He may be right but the way he goes about it imposes major constraints on its effectiveness. He believes firmly in involving his department in making this decision and already has a mandate from his headteacher (administratively regulated). He draws up a schedule of meetings for his staff to consider their views and expects them to attend because they are held in 'directed time' (compulsory). The department meets and is persuaded to work together to implement a mandate over which it has no control (implementation-oriented and fixed in time and space). Following the discussions the new reporting system was introduced (predictable). Why did the head of department bother? He knew what he wanted, how he wanted to do it, and when. The departmental meetings may have resulted in fine-tuning the new system but little more. He could, however, when questioned say that he had held wide-ranging discussions with his department and that there was agreement about the new system. Change had occurred in the structure of how learning was evaluated but it is unlikely to have resulted in a significant change in the way teachers operated within their classes. The solution was contrived in the same way as the collaboration.

A *collaborative culture* is one in which people, not structures, are the agents of change. Hargreaves (1994, pp.192–3) identifies five main features of collaborative culture. Firstly, it is *spontaneous*. History teachers in a department have discussed informally in the staffroom their concern about the underachievement of certain students in Year 8 and decide they want to meet formally to consider the problem. In this situation the head of history acts as an administrative support, perhaps scheduling arrangements or offering to cover classes so that meetings can occur during the school day. Spontaneity does not mean an anarchic approach to the problem or that there is no administrative structuring. It means that collaborative relationships have developed from a concern about the learning of history. Secondly, it is a *voluntary* culture that has emerged as of perceived value to the teachers rather than as a result of administrative diktat or compulsion. The consequence of this is that the head of department ends up with a group of teachers who want to work together in a productive and enjoyable spirit. Thirdly, collaborative cultures are *development-oriented*. It is the individual members of the history department who have established the purposes and tasks of working together rather than the head of history making decisions with departmental validation to make it happen. Fourthly, collaborative cultures are *pervasive across time and space*. Most history departments operate on the basis of scheduled meetings, often built into the year plan. These may form part of a collaborative culture but they do not govern the arrangements for working together. In collaborative cultures, much of the way teachers work together is almost unnoticed. It is the informal chat, the offers of support, the suggestions of new ideas and sharing of problems that are its characteristics. Teachers spend most of their time in the classroom and collaborative cultures allow them to build on that experience in developing effective change mechanisms. Finally, it is *unpredictable*. Its outcomes are often uncertain. This could put it at odds with heads of department who have a more centralised and controlling perception of their role. In addition, I would suggest that collaborative cultures are *less threatening* to individual history teachers.

This is not to say that collaborative cultures are without their share of problems. They may well become restricted with history teachers fastening on to 'safe' activities rather than reflecting on the purposes of what they are doing, reflecting on their practice and challenging each others' assumptions. As Hargreaves (1994, p.195) says, 'Collegiality can be reduced to congeniality'. Where a collaborative culture has emerged heads of history can build on the collective strengths and confidence of departmental staff who are able to interact assertively with the need for change.

Most history departments operate through a combination of these two types of collaboration. There may be occasions where contrived collaboration is necessary to 'get things done'. Earley and Fletcher-Campbell (1989, pp.19–44) show clearly that heads of department spend only a small proportion of their week on work associated with staff development, curriculum evaluation, liaison with other curriculum areas and participation on whole-school working parties. Far more time is spent on routine administration like examination entries, cover arrangements, room allocation and stationery. Collaborative cultures can become inactive or at least non-productive in achieving change. Heads of department need to apply their leadership skills to a collaborative culture to ensure that it is productive.

Change and the history department

It's the beginning of a new school year. The head of the history department has returned bronzed from a holiday in the sun. She's had much time to think about the next year, a process aided by a nagging fear that GCSE and A level results are going to be poor. The results are as bad as expected and the Curriculum Deputy is breathing down her neck for an explanation. She's unhappy with the results and wants to do something about them. And that means change. But the same thing happened a year ago and, after many planning meetings and discussions, she thought she'd persuaded her department to change the ways in which they taught examination classes. All that time and effort with no tangible result. As managers of history departments we have all been there. Changes we thought had put down firm foundations prove to be ineffective. Why? The illusion of change in the history curriculum, of the ways in which we teach and of the learning we expect of students are common features of developments in schools. Changes look good but they are often cosmetic rather than real, a case of innovation without change.

This is not surprising. There is an inherent tension between the essentially conservative history teacher and the dynamics associated with the continuous change necessary to achieve and maintain quality student learning. This is a basic problem that has to be resolved. Innovation without change is an expression of how continuous change is watered-down. It is unrealistic to expect that introducing innovation into a situation that is not structured to engage in change will do anything but blunt the edge of reform and give it a bad name. Breaking through this impasse means heads of history seeing themselves and being seen by their departments as experts in the dynamics of change. This is not a case of tinkering or hoping that change will happen or believing that you can accomplish it by playing safe. Achieving a greater capacity for change must be explicit and pursued collaboratively in an all out manner.

A prime imperative

Change in history starts from a single moral imperative: all change must have an impact upon the ability of students to develop their mastery of learning. Too often managers of history presume that this *is* the case. It must, however, be made explicit. Goodlad (1990) singles out three elements that lie at the hub of good teaching:

1. *Teaching should facilitate critical enculturation.* 'Schools are major players in developing educated people who acquire an understanding for truth, beauty and justice against which to judge their own and society's virtues and imperfections...' (pp.48–9). History teachers have a major role to play in the development of critical awareness, providing students with the skills necessary to make valid judgements.

2. *Teaching should provide access to knowledge.* Although some writers like Michael Barber see this as increasingly not the case, Goodlad suggests that '[Schools are] the only institutions in our society specifically charged with providing for the young a disciplined encounter with all the subject matter of human conversion...' (p.49) An understanding of the past is central to student understanding of their place in the modern world and without this temporal perspective they cannot claim to be prepared for their place in adult society.

3. *Teaching should build an effective connection with the learner.* 'The epistemology of teaching must encompass a pedagogy that goes far beyond the mechanics of teaching. It must combine generalizable principles of teaching, subject specific instruction and sensitivity to the pervasive human qualities and potentials always involved.' (pp.49–50)

These three elements, as we have already seen in Chapter 3, are at the heart of achieving quality student learning.

To make this happen *every* teacher in a history department must strive to be an effective agent of change. Fullan (1993, p.12) has identified four parallel core capacities necessary for building a greater capacity for change within individual teachers and across departments.

Individual	Departmental
Personal vision-building	Shared vision-building
Enquiry	Organisational structures, norms and practices of enquiry
Mastery	Focus on organisational development and know-how or towards a learning organisation
Collaboration	Collaborative work cultures

The objective of managers of history is to achieve a dual approach working simultaneously on individual and departmental levels. Without this, change can become stilted, unsure and ineffective.

Changing the individual teacher

History departments are abstractions. Change in history takes place not because an organisation wills it but because people, individually and in collaboration, recognise the need for change. Changing structures without changing people will result in cosmetic change. *Personal vision-building* is the starting point for any attempt to develop change successfully. Shared vision is important in the long run but to be effective teachers have to have something to share. Vision is not the preserve of leaders alone and articulating and making explicit what history teachers see as their personal vision forces them to reflect on what they are doing. Facing your personal vision can be a painful, discomforting process for teachers. Discussions with a group of teachers in early 1994 threw up the following:

'I came into teaching because I believed I could change things. It's been a disappointing process.' (male teacher, aged twenty-seven, four years' experience)

'I thought I could make a difference.' (male teacher, aged thirty-two, ten years' experience)

'History was a passion I wanted to convey to others.' (female teacher, aged twenty-eight, five years' experience)

'Teaching children to learn history but it all seems to have got muddled up by successive changes in the curriculum and all the paperwork and pointless meetings.' (male teacher, aged forty, eighteen years' experience)

These were the *least* negative responses and my experience of many conferences and long discussions lead me to conclude that they are commonly held views. It seems other things get in the way of enabling students to achieve quality learning. By restoring student learning to the heart of individual vision, all the paraphernalia that is teaching history today can be seen in a new and arguably more positive context. Teachers, like students, must be motivated by what they do. Personal vision gives meaning to work. It should be articulated not just as a private and self-centred process but within its social dimension, especially with regard to working effectively with others in the history team. It must be pursued explicitly and aggressively.

The second element, *enquiry*, means 'internalizing norms, habits and techniques for continuous learning' (Fullan, 1993, p.15). This means a persistent questioning by history teachers of their pedagogy so that its quality may be continually improved. Observation of colleagues' lessons by all members of a history department is particularly valuable. It allows a focus on a particular aspect of teaching, for example, the amount of time a teacher spends talking to the class or the effectiveness of group work. It is also useful preparation for OFSTED inspection, getting both students and staff used to having someone else in their classes. For example, a Year 7 lesson on the Roman invasion of Britain taught by a non-specialist was observed by the head of a humanities department. The focus was on how effectively the teacher conveyed the content to her class and how well the students understood this content. The head of humanities identified three particular issues. Firstly, the non-specialist seems less than happy with the content of the lesson and approached it very tentatively. Secondly, the students' participation in the lesson was low with few questions being asked by the teacher of the class. Thirdly, when given ten short answer questions to do at the end of the lesson only three students out of thirty got full marks and half the students scored less than five. The head of humanities also talked to students who were invited to give their views on what they had learned. This was followed up at the end of the school day with a thirty-minute meeting. As a result the head of humanities was able to help the non-specialist with her understanding of the content, suggesting alternative ways, like the use of timelines and diagrams, of enabling students to learn what happened. She also encouraged the teacher to involve students more effectively in the lesson as an important means of motivation. The consequence was personal change for the teacher and improved quality of learning for students as she revised her teaching approach to the subject for a lesson later in the week, with markedly improved learning results. This process, akin to Schon's notion of the 'reflective practitioner', is critical at all stages of teachers' careers but particularly for the novice. Through this a persistent enquiring quality can be inculcated in individual history teachers, allowing them to update their personal visions.

The third component of changing the individual teacher is the capacity for *mastery*. Change does not take place because people think about new ideas and skills but because of the different ways in which they act. Personal mastery is grounded in skills and competence but it goes beyond them and means approaching teaching history from a creative or proactive as opposed to a reactive viewpoint (Senge, 1990). It means clarifying what is important to us as history teachers (the issue of our purpose and vision). A point made by many teachers is that we spend so much time dealing with the day-to-day problems of teaching history that we often forget why we are teaching it in the first place. It is not enough to be exposed to new ideas, we have to know where they fit in our teaching. This places a considerable responsibility on heads of history to manage change effectively for each member of their departments. History teachers, finally, need to ask themselves, how much can we develop if we keep to ourselves? This means effective *collaboration* to form productive mentoring and peer relationships within departments and team building. Personal development, especially if oriented towards enquiry, goes hand-in-hand with collaboration.

Personal development, grounded in vision, enquiry, mastery and collaboration, is not without its cost. The four elements can produce anxieties in teachers. Some teachers find being observed by colleagues stressful and find it difficult to respond positively to the outcomes of those observations. Other finds the need to take risks and experience the unknown in teaching history very difficult. They prefer the certainty of what they already do to the possibility of improving their students' ability to learn by using new pedagogical strategies. Rosenholtz (1989) found that teachers in departments that used these techniques for personal development not only became better at what they did but also more confident in their ability to achieve creative breakthroughs in student learning. These difficulties are a necessary part of the process of establishing quality learning and of 'liberating' the management of learning history. Peters (1993, pp.757–8) suggests that we are all students in a learning environment. This is certainty true of teachers if they want to achieve higher levels of quality learning in their students. So Peters suggests:

> ...get turned on. Or follow your bliss (vision?) or whatever. Vacuous advice? Perhaps. But the practical implication is this: In a knowledge-based economy, you must – to survive – add some special value, be distinctively good at something. And the truth is, we usually only get good at stuff we like. If you love skiing and you're a newly minted MBA, look to get a job in some sporting-related industry that lets you turn skiing to professional advantage. Ain't nobody gonna take care of you on the job in a big company anymore: It's not dog-eat-dog out there, it's skill-eat-skill. If you're not skilled/motivated/passionate about something, you're in trouble.

The implication of this for history teachers is twofold: '[As a history teacher] you must retrain yourself – constantly and forever...You must, by hook or by crook, keep at it.' 'The biggest risk is not taking risks and getting pigeonholed.' (Peters, 1993, p.758). Changing the teaching of history so that quality learning is the outcome is not something that can or will be successfully imposed from above. Heads of history cannot implement change alone.

Changing the history department

Change is usually a tangle of conflicting and contradictory elements and is often unpredictable. Finding solutions means developing better ways of thinking about and dealing with this situation. Pascale (1990) indicates that productive educational change drifts somewhere between over-control and chaos, a view suggested in Peters (1987). Before chaos theory, scientists taught us that big effects were generally the result of big causes. Now they suggest that small changes in initial conditions can have enormous consequences. However, management in schools can become an invention that produces gains in organisational efficiency so great that it eventually destroys organisational efficiency. This loss of effectiveness comes from ignoring the commitment to people. The structure and modifying the structure become increasingly important and managers lose sight of their initial imperatives. Over-planning and over-control by heads of department can leave little room for teachers to become self-motivated. So how can we ensure that history departments change so that they can deliver effective student learning?

It is essential to recognise from the start that it is quite normal for change to be complex, dynamic and unpredictable. Heads of history have to take account of a whole range of variables that may influence a problem. Take staffing a department. As a head of department I may want teacher A to teach classes 1, 2, 3 and 4, giving her a variety of experiences from the most to the least able to broaden her expertise in the classroom, while teacher B I know is happier with able classes in Years 7 to 11 and with A level. What I want and what the timetabler can accommodate is another matter. Other variables intervene. The head of maths wants mixed ability groups and I want history to be taught in setted groups but maths and history are timetabled at the same time. Teacher B also teaches business studies and this is timetabled against his existing A level classes. And so on. The solution I end up with is a 'best-fit' solution that doesn't satisfy my teachers or me. This simple example will be familiar to all heads of history. The critical questions I have to find solutions to are: what effect could this solution have upon the effective learning of students, what effect will it have upon my teachers and what impact will it have on the motivation of both? Many heads of history would see this as an organisational problem. The reality, I am suggesting, is that it is a people problem.

Fullan (1993, pp.21–2) suggests that what is needed is a new paradigm of dynamic change and that there are eight basic lessons which teachers need to consider. The remainder of this section will consider these lessons and suggest ways in which they can be applied to history departments.

- **Lesson One**: *You can't mandate what matters*. The more complex the change the less you can force it. What matters when heads of history are introducing change are the skills, creative thinking and commitment of members of their departments. I can write policies, establish standards and monitor staff and student performance but this is not sufficient and the more I try to specify them the narrower the goals become. I can adopt the latest ideas about teaching or multicultural education or special needs but unless deeper changes in thinking and skills by all members of the department take place then they will have a limited impact on student learning. The main problem heads of history have to face is not resistance to change, though this exists in all departments in one form or another, but the existence of too many policies adopted uncritically and superficially. New ideas require commitment and thought and these cannot be mandated. Unless this occurs, change will be seen as marginal to the real purpose of teaching and student learning.

- **Lesson Two**: *Change is a journey not a blueprint*. Change is non-linear, loaded with uncertainty and excitement and sometimes perverse. Heads of history cannot plan the outcomes of change with any real precision. There are simply too many variables and unknowns. I may know what I would like to be the outcome and have my blueprint for implementation but I cannot know for certain that this will be the eventual conclusion. Four heads of history decided that they would buy a common textbook for their Year 9 students, having first considered the alternatives with their departments. Negotiations with the publisher led to a significant cost reduction. All students used the book but in one school the department discovered that the book, excellent though it was, did not really cater for the needs of the less able. The original scheme of work therefore had to be modified to take this into account. The original planning had been sound but had the head of department concerned adopted the blueprint approach and had he not been prepared to alter the framework for teaching then the outcome would have been a reduction in the ability of some students to learn effectively. In this case, though having to change was frustrating, there was something the department could do about it. In other cases this may not be the case and you won't be able to do anything at all. Now that's real frustration and departments have to learn to contend with both the positive and negative forces of change. If they can do that then they will be able to develop quality learning by their students.

- **Lesson Three**: *Problems are our friends*. Problems are inevitable and you can't learn without them. History departments will not develop effective responses to complex situations unless they actively seek and confront the real problems that may be difficult to solve. Take the problem of timetabling staff mentioned above. The head of department cannot ignore or deny that there is a problem and the teachers concerned should not treat it as an occasion for blame and defence. Louis and Miles (1990) found that least successful departments engaged in 'shallow coping' by doing nothing, using delaying tactics, doing things the usual way and thus increasing pressure on teachers, while more successful departments went deeper to explore underlying causes and to find more creative answers. By immersing themselves openly in the problem departments may then be able to come up with inventive solutions. The focus is on *they*. The problem is not simply the head of department's or the individual teacher's but one that crosses the management divide. In fact a creative solution is unlikely to be found if there is a management divide. Collaboration is the key.

  Heads of history like to say that things are 'going smoothly' or that 'there aren't any problems'. This often means that either little is being attempted or that superficial or insignificant change is being traded for meaningful attempts at change. Effective change is about confusion and conflict and about asking discomforting questions until the sources of problems are laid bare. Problems allow us to change and in that sense they are our friends but only if something is done about them.

- **Lesson Four**: *Vision and strategic planning come later*. Premature visions and planning blind. Vision-driven change is still seen as the key to successful management by heads of history. First, create and establish *your* departmental vision. Then communicate that vision to *your* department and, as a consequence, build commitment to the vision. Finally organise *your* teachers and what they do to correspond to *your* vision. This may appear sound and logical but it is increasingly seen by business as wrong. Most visions of this type are the head of department's and, at best, command compliance not commitment from teachers. It implies that it is possible to have a vision of change while Lesson Two shows clearly that change is a journey rather than a blueprint. What we need are *shared* visions that departments as a whole are committed to because they reflect the personal visions of teachers. The focus again is on people not structures. It is perfectly plausible for heads of history to develop their own visions but they will be without ownership by history departments unless they have been subjected to a great deal of reflection and development. Visions emerge from action. They do not precede it.

The same arguments can be deployed against strategic planning. The departmental development plan is now integral to the lives of heads of history, produced annually and almost invariably put in the filing cabinet until the next round of planning when it will be evaluated. It is a paper exercise that looks good for OFSTED and may play an important part in whether your department can bid successfully for additional resourcing. What is its value? It certainly focuses the minds of departments but spending too much time and energy on planning, even with built-in flexibility, is a mistake. No 'plan' can take account of the perversity and relentlessness of change in schools. An annual history department plan was submitted in January 1994 complete with costings and priorities. Top priority concerned making decisions about a new GCSE course but then Dearing changed the rules. Second priority concerned A level and the need for more resources but then twenty-five students opted to take the course rather than the usual ten. Third priority was on choosing a new text for Year 9 less able students and then came Dearing so publishers delayed publication of new texts. All that planning and where did it get me? This is not to say that planning is unimportant but, like vision, it needs to be shared and not to distract teachers from their *own* possibilities.

Pilot projects provide an excellent way of creating and clarifying vision and planning. These allow teachers to try things out to see whether they lead to increased student learning. A history department decided that the existing provision for A level did not allow students to transfer their demonstrable learning abilities in class into high quality examination results. Various solutions were suggested at departmental meetings, especially changing to a new A level course. The head of department was not convinced that this would lead to the desired improvements and she suggested that this should be delayed for a year while other strategies were tried. This made good sense to her as change on this scale required large quantities of new resources and there was no guarantee that the necessary finance would be made available or that it would improve results. She suggested, therefore, that the A level teachers tried using different teaching strategies to develop student skill under examination conditions and shared the conclusions with their colleagues. One teacher adopted a programme of testing under examination conditions linked to developing student revision strategies. A second used her free time to discuss work with each student on a fortnightly basis. The head of department helped students to order their notes with the examination in mind. The consequence was a substantial improvement in student results. This allowed the head of department to initiate discussion about changing the syllabus, not in a spirit of 'crisis' but as a valid pedagogical strategy. There will still be debate and unresolved issues but it placed the department in a far better position to pursue further change with greater clarity of purpose and, as a result, with shared vision.

By reversing the traditionally held views about vision and planning it is possible for history departments to achieve deeper and more powerful shared visions that inspire committed action on a daily basis. Combined with the view of change as a journey it brings the prime imperative of achieving quality student learning to the fore and takes change off the written page and into the classroom.

● **Lesson Five**: *Individualism and collectivism must have equal power.* There are no one-sided solutions to isolation and groupthink. Heads of history face two basic types of problems in running their departments. *Convergent* problems deal with distinct, quantifiable problems that can generally be resolved by reason, like producing statistical information on examination results or putting students into classes. Solving a convergent problem literally eliminates it. *Divergent* problems, like deciding a new examination syllabus or reorganising the teaching of special needs, are not quantifiable, do not lend themselves to a single solution and cannot be permanently eliminated.

On one side there are history teachers and on the other history departments. Problems are addressed and sometimes satisfactorily resolved by a combination of the two. 'Productive education change is a process of overcoming isolation while not succumbing to groupthink.' (Fullan, 1993, p.33). Teaching can be an 'isolated' profession. We are in *our* classrooms teaching history to *our* students. This is a process that may allow conservatism and resistance to change to fester. It makes history teachers defensive. This is a problem heads of history need to be aware of since it imposes a ceiling on the enquiry and development of the individual and, as a result, may limit solutions to problems to the experience of the individual. Collaborative approaches do allow this sense of isolation to be mitigated but, if pushed too far, may lead to groupthink, what Fullan (1993, p.34) defines as the 'uncritical conformity to the group, unthinking acceptance of the latest solution and the suppression of individual dissent'. This can itself limit change. What is necessary is a balance between the positive aspects of individualism, like the capacity to work independently, and the strengths of collaborative work. Heads of history need to recognise and value the diversity of their teaching staff just as teachers must acknowledge the diversity of student experience.

- **Lesson Six**: *Neither centralisation nor decentralisation work.* Both top-down and bottom-up strategies are necessary. Centralisation tends towards over-control; decentralisation verges towards chaos and uncertainty. Top-down solutions, as the original National Curriculum in history clearly demonstrates, rarely work. Decentralised solutions also fail because groups turn in on themselves, become preoccupied with their own problems and consequently fail to see the broader picture. Successful change is a combination of consensus above and pressure from below. In history departments this means that policies developed exclusively by heads of department will fail in the same way as leaving history teachers to make policy decisions will fail. In a collaborative department this situation should not arise since pressure from teachers for change, for example, in the way groups are organised for teaching in terms of a mixed ability/setting debate, can occur within a consensus framework of a solution grounded in what will lead to quality learning for students.

- **Lesson Seven**: *Connection with the wider environment is critical for success.* The best organisations learn externally as well as internally. History departments are themselves part of a broader framework of faculties and schools. Heads of department should be aware of this. They attend the whole-school policy meetings. Collaboration exists across departments and curriculums within schools and with the wider environment. History teachers still need to focus on making a difference to the learning of their own students but failure to recognise that this has a whole-school dimension can act as a block to that learning. A 'balkanisation' of subjects in the whole-school curriculum (in fact in this situation the whole-school curriculum is something of a misnomer) leads to intense competition between subjects for time, resources and staffing that diverts attention away from the need to recognise the holistic nature of the curriculum and student learning.

Take coursework. Most subjects now have a coursework component at GCSE, as do and an increasing number of post-16 courses. The history department has a responsibility for creating working conditions that will be most effective in helping all students learn. Not just in history but in mathematics, English, science and so on. This means not just being aware of what learning students are expected to do across the curriculum but being responsive to the needs of other departments. History may be the sun around which teachers orbit but for students there are other suns and other orbits that need to be satisfied.

- **Lesson Eight**: *Every person is a change agent.* Change is too important to leave to the experts, personal mind set and mastery are the ultimate protection. Successful history departments are collaborative organisations in which there is debate, disagreement, change, failure, risk, commitment and creativity. Continuous change is something every member of a department needs to be committed to. This cannot be left any longer to heads of department working on their own. Each teacher in history departments has a responsibility to ensure that change will occur. In fact without this change will simply not happen. If history teachers are going to improve the ability of their students to learn history effectively then we have to go beyond our prime imperative and change. The individual teacher is the engine that powers change, who pushes for change, debates and disagrees about change. Teachers, individually and collaboratively, can make a difference for students learning history.

This analysis of change and the history department is not a comfortable one but I suggest it is exciting. It provides an alternative to existing approaches to change in history. It recognises the polarities of over-control and chaos and seeks to use the tensions between them creatively to achieve a state of continuous change in which history teachers and history departments find dynamic solutions to the problems that face them. It recognises the creative and complex tensions of managing change successfully. It is a solution that values both the individual and the history team, which acknowledges that it is the combination of individuals and groups that makes a difference and sees quality student learning as *the* prime justification for innovation.

Project teams: the way forward in history?

Schools only really began to grapple with the complexities of business management techniques in the late 1970s and early 1980s when the increasing demands made on schools, especially the development of the notion of 'the school in the market place', first appeared. Progress has been fitful and HMI commented in DES, (1988b, p.6) that 'in many schools the role of middle management, particularly that of heads of department, was under-developed.' We have fortunately gone beyond the stage when management of history departments was seen simply as a set of techniques and procedures applied by the head of department to the managed (teachers and students) in order to control change in a direction considered to be appropriate by the head of department. Or have we? Prescriptive techniques and leadership styles still dominate management approaches in many departments even if there is a significant element of contrived collaboration. This section addresses how collaborative cultures can be converted into effective team management of student learning in history.

Why teams?

The organisational complexities of departments makes it very difficult for teachers to understand with any degree of certainty the full history learning programme of all the students. Heads of department are supposed to have the overview or, as Drucker (1968, p.409) says, '[they] must, so to speak, keep [their] noses to the grindstone while lifting [their] eyes to the hills' but this too is increasingly difficult. A hierarchical or middle management approach to managing history departments is no longer adequate. As Peters (1994, p.756) says 'middle managers, as we have known them, are cooked geese'. What we need are teams of staff working with heads of history as consultants to build a collaborative culture so that we may move beyond hierarchies towards creating projects focused on the effective learning of students. It is this 'product' that is of fundamental importance in the management of history and on which the success or failure of teams will be decided.

Project teams are functional groups. They have a task or series of tasks to complete. They will consist of a number of individuals within history departments, on occasions the whole department. They will be guided by a team leader who accepts overall responsibility for carrying the project through to completion. This may be the head of history but it could equally well be another member of the department with the departmental head acting simply as one of its members. Some teams may be temporary with limited tasks such as planning a course module or a Year 11 trip. Others may be of a more permanent nature like the team responsible for the Year 7 course, though membership of the team will change through time. Some will be established by heads of department (part of their prescriptive role of contriving collaboration) while others will emerge from discussions, often informal, among members of history departments through a shared collaborative culture. Outsiders, for example heads of special needs, may be invited to join teams when their particular expertise is needed but, in most circumstances, teams in history departments will tend to consist of staff from those departments.

The notion of project teams has been explored particularly in business (for example, Hastings, 1986, and Adair, 1987) and in education (for example, Bell, 1992, and Tansley, 1989). Bell suggests (Table 4.2, p.46) that the benefits of teamwork in schools are: agreeing aims, clarifying roles, sharing expertise and skills, maximising use of resources, motivating, supporting and encouraging members of the team, improved relationship within the staff group, encouraging decision-making, increasing participation, realising individual potential, improving communication, increasing knowledge and understanding, and reducing stress and anxiety. Teams are more powerful learning entities than individual history teachers seeking to learn and change on their own. They provide an environment where ideas about change can be articulated, tested, refined and examined against the needs of history departments and within the context of learning to change with others. Murgatroyd and Morgan, (1993, p.142) argue that to be effective team-based activities need to be based on 'the needs of the team, the needs of the individuals within the team and the needs of the organization.' They also suggest a pragmatic reason if sustainable quality improvement over time is to be established. They maintain that it has to be independent of any particular individual. 'Many excellent initiatives die when their champion leaves the school...innovations that are team-owned and team-sustained are far less likely to be dependent on an individual champion.' This reinforces the notion of shared collaborative culture as a basis for effective quality change over the contrived collaboration often associated with a charismatic or forceful leader.

Project teams allow history teachers to become more focused in what they do and consequently more organised. Tansley (1989, p.59) found that around 40 per cent of principals mentioned the benefits to students arising from the operation of course teams and nearly 20 per cent also felt it led staff to accept change more willingly. Work becomes a dialogue in which the department is a collection of ever-forming, ever-dissolving, ever-changing, multi-functional skilled project teams. It is this 'structure' that is at the heart of Fullan's notion of the paradigm of change. Peters (1994, p.472) sums up this situation: 'Work as dialogue, shared minds and the floating crap games of project teams (of insiders and outsiders) "tied" together by soul of some sort – that's the mostly elusive "stuff" that adds up to "beyond hierarchy"...' Teams are accountable for what they do but paradoxically individuals are given more autonomy for what they do collectively and are more dependent on each other as team members.

Establishing project teams

A linguistic change is spreading across history departments. Heads of history are being replaced by history co-ordinators. Is this a simple case of old wine in new bottles? Has the change in title been accompanied by a change in management style and a move towards project teams? Well, following Tansley (1989, p.202), it all depends on your perspective. She found that, when determining the effectiveness of teams, college principals highlighted regular meetings, productive team work and successful achievement of aims. Course teachers stressed student outcomes and enjoyment of courses, whereas co-ordinators cited the enthusiasm of team members, achievement of course aims and favourable student reaction.

Several members of a history department are concerned about the effectiveness of the Year 8 course. They point to what they see as the inflexibility of the existing structure with students being rushed through the National Curriculum units to ensure that all the prescribed topics are covered. They argue that this leads to student demotivation and point to poor test results as evidence for their view. The head of department, who had written the Year 8 course, recognises their anxieties and judges that she should allow those concerned to formulate an alternative solution to the problem. She suggests that they form a small group to look at the issue and report back to the whole department the following month. She has recognised the need for a project team. If it is to achieve its objective, there is remarkably consistent research on the characteristics of successful project teams (see Murgatroyd and Morgan, 1993, pp.143–7, and Hastings, 1986, pp.105–13):

- *It will have a shared sense of purpose and vision.* As in this case, this often precedes the structural creation of a project team. The teachers already have a common understanding of what is expected in terms of outcome and the team is focused and generates dynamic creativity as a result of this common understanding.

- *There will be open communication.* There should be no hidden agenda. The head of history must recognise that she may have to change her views on the Year 8 course and should not see the establishment of the project team as a way of heading off and diffusing criticism. There should be a lot of direct, open and honest talk.

- *There will be trust and mutuality.* This is not automatic and will certainly be harmed if the head of history takes a defensive position on the Year 8 course. What binds the team is its sense of responsibility both for the process it is going through and for the project.

- *There will be useful creative conflict.* This is unavoidable and essential if the team is to reach as creative a solution to the problem as possible. Conflict is inevitable even when a team starts from an agreed position as in this case.

- *There will be appropriate working methods.* Many history teachers point to poor communications, lack of consultation and the waste of time inherent in departmental meetings as among the most stressful aspects of their work. These stem either from a prescriptive or leader-oriented approach to management by heads of history. Project teams should not fall into this situation. If they do, the team will not function effectively. The team in this case consists of four members and it establishes its own working pattern: there is full access to information about Year 8; the team knows who is doing what and by when; minutes of meetings are kept, especially about what has been agreed and about what there is still disagreement. This approach is cost-effective. Many departments do some or all of these things poorly. It is valuable to estimate the cost in staff time of team meetings. For example, costing staff time at a nominal £10 per hour means that a team meeting would cost £40 per hour. If no decisions have been reached then effectively that is £40 wasted.

- *There will be appropriate leadership.* Most project teams will have a chairperson responsible for the routines of meetings, preparing minutes and agendas and ensuring that issues are followed up and dealt with. This may be the head of history is she is one of the team but this need not be the case. The project leader's role is facilitative, not one of domination.

- *There will be regular review and reflection.* It is essential that the team stops working on a project from time to time and reviews what it has done and its working methods. This allows the question of whether the team could work more effectively to be dealt with.

- *Individual development will be encouraged.* The effectiveness of a project team is a result of the sum of its varied parts. The team reviewing the Year 8 course relies on the knowledge and expertise of each of its four members. Without this, individual ownership and commitment to decisions is reduced and the coherence of the team can be threatened. Hastings (1986, p.106) gives the following example: "'We came up with that idea and we agreed it", said one of our teamworking course participants "and that means I did too. It's my idea but it's ours too. And that feels good!'"

- *There will be sound links with other teams.* Teams do not work in isolation. Similar groups may have been established in other subjects, English for example, whose work may impact upon the Year 8 team. Where this is the case effective teams link themselves with other teams, sharing ideas and concerns and recognising that facilitating change in history may mean accommodating the work and ideas of other teams.

Project teams, once formed, will not be effective from day one. Murgatroyd and Morgan (1993) and Thomas and Woods (1994) identify similar stages in the development of effective teams – see Figure 4.1.

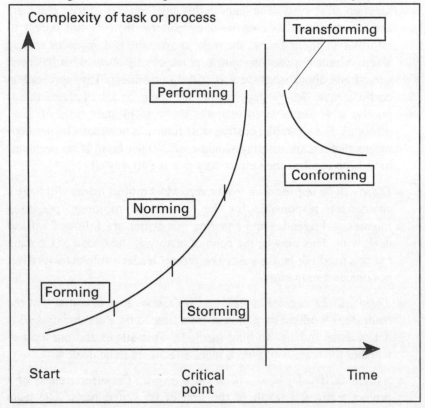

Figure 4.1 Stages of team development

[derived from Truckman and Jensen (1977), reproduced in Murgatroyd and Morgan (1993, p.150)]

The first stage is referred to as *forming*. The team is underdeveloped and, according to Thomas and Woods (1994, p.133), 'The manager needs to allocate, control and monitor, otherwise things do not get done. An authoritarian style of management is essential at this stage.' Certainly the project team needs to be kept on task but if the head of history never relaxes her grasp the group cannot settle in and develop into an effective team. Where a collaborative culture already exists, forming the team can be relatively easy. Where it does not, this stage can be a difficult one. The team can be suspicious of the real nature of the project and behave with a degree of insecurity about the task and their own roles within the team. There will be guarded exchanges of information and one-sided attempts to establish positions.

The individuals in the project team then begin to find their own feet, understand or define the overall purpose of the task and need to define exactly how they fit it. This leads to the second or *storming* stage where conflict emerges over roles and tasks. Strong, often antagonistic, feelings appear and the team as a whole and team members individually feel considerable vulnerability and uncertainty. Working through issues rather than avoiding them is essential at this stage if the team is to become stronger. Things can only get better but rarely without some blood on the carpet. Through this process of purging the project team will either find its own identity or will collapse.

The team gradually consolidates its position and establishes its own identity with norms of behaviour and process, thus reaching the *norming* stage of its development. There is an open exchange of information and problems, a sharing within a collaborative culture, with feelings and concerns expressed largely in non-antagonistic ways. There is a reduction of pointless conflict. This allows the team to start *performing*. Everyone simply gets on with the job and people problems are handled in a matter-of-fact way without fuss. The team then becomes effective and efficient in understanding how best to meet the challenges it has set itself.

Vulnerability re-emerges at this stage. The project team, now mature and confident in itself and its members, has to make a decision between *conforming* (settling into a low-risk route) or *transforming* through re-examination of its work in the light of the need for constant change. Evidence from five history departments demonstrates that most teams opt for the safe route of conforming. This is a comfortable solution in which change slows down, energy declines and performance levels drift into adequate but not optimum levels. Renewal of the project team is essential at this point so that it can change its work from acceptable to outstanding.

Project teams are the building blocks of organisations. High-performing history departments are collections of high-quality teams.

Project teams are the key channels for meeting demanding and tough goals and maintaining effectiveness over time. Mature teams reflect a collaborative culture and unleash the energies and expertise of history teachers. They allow outrageous goals to be examined, accepted or rejected, implemented and evaluated. They are often initially an uncomfortable even a shocking means of generating change. They empower individuals and groups in ways that traditional management techniques, grounded in notions of contrived collaboration, do not. They are the best way of achieving the prime imperative of all history departments, to improve the learning of history by students.

Making change stick

Much has been written about managing change in schools (for example, the very useful and readable studies by Fullan, 1991, Newton and Tarrant, 1992, and Whitaker, 1993). This chapter has suggested that change is most effectively accomplished where there is a shared collaborative culture within history departments and where there is clarity as to the prime imperative of any change process. The result is organisational flexibility and real commitment on the part of history teachers as well as a creative uncertainty as to what they are doing. This challenges the long-held view of teachers that what is necessary for effective change is a regulatory order and certainty, generally prescribed by the head of department. This may have been adequate in the all-embracing cosy world of the old tripartite system but it is no longer so today in the realities of the educational market and with intense competition for student numbers. Certainty no longer exists for history teachers. It isn't simply a case of making change stick or managing changes simply to survive but of recognising the reality of managing departments in the 1990s. Change is no longer a case simply of carrying out particular tasks but a process of continuous regeneration, of reordering history departments, of establishing effective networks of history teachers in teams so that they can deliver effective student learning. Unless the behaviour of history teachers changes nothing will change, departments will ossify and become unable to meet the challenges that face them. The learning process is the key to achieving change both in ourselves and in our departments. Today what matters is quality.

CHAPTER 5

Managing Learning History

Recognizing is one thing. Energizing people to do something is quite something else. There is only a finite amount of energy available in an organization and if, for example, all that energy is poured into finding ways of rewarding and reinforcing current behaviour, products and practices, even the most energetic chief executive is going to have an uphill struggle if he sees the need to change things.

Plant (1987, p.66)

All enterprises – hospitals, industries, banks for example – are organised round, and for the convenience of, the 'production' function. Hospitals are chiefly structured to support doctors, surgery and laboratory work. Industries are fashioned to maximise factory efficiency. Banks are largely the product of the most advantageous operational practices. On the whole, their practices benefit the customer. The patient generally gets well, the computer or the car usually works, bank accounts are serviced. History departments too provide quality services. There are, however, significant differences between providing quality services in manufacturing and in teaching history. Firstly, services provided by history departments are *intangible* because they are performances rather than objects. Many of the services history teachers provide cannot be measured, listed, tested or validated before delivery to ensure quality. Secondly, history departments have customers with *varied* needs. Within any classroom, the particular learning needs of individual students will be different and parents, as customers, often have different needs from their children. Thirdly, the production and consumption of services provided by history departments are *inseparable,* unlike those in manufacturing industries. Quality cannot be engineered into the product at the planning stage and then delivered intact to students. Indeed, the product is a result of the symbiotic relationship between teachers and students with the latter intimately involved in the process. Judgement on the quality of what is provided by history departments is a result of an assessment of the outcomes of the service and an evaluation of the ways in which the service is delivered. The previous chapters have considered ways in which the quality of student learning – the end-product of the service history departments provide – can be improved and made more effective. I have suggested that a collaborative approach by teachers and students is central to this process. In this chapter I intend to consider how the successful learning of history can be enhanced by heads of history and their departments through the medium of Total Quality Management (TQM).

TQM and learning history

TQM presupposes that quality is the outcome of all the activities that take place within an organisation. It assumes that all functions and all employees participate in the improvement process and that organisations need both quality systems and a quality culture (Morgan and Murgatroyd, 1994, p.8). This means five things for history departments:

1. TQM involves everything that history departments do, helping to determine their status and reputation within schools and outside.

2. TQM is a total system of quality improvement in which history departments make decisions based on the collection of data rather than subjectively through opinion and impression.

3. The total quality provided by history departments includes not just the quality of the service that students and other clients receive but everything departments do internally to maintain continuing performance improvement.

4. TQM presumes that quality is the outcome of all activities that take place within departments and that all the functions of departments lead to improvement in quality.

5. TQM affects everyone in history departments. It assumes that every job and process that occurs within departments is carried out successfully, first time and every time.

Total Quality Management is about the management systems used by history departments to assure quality and about the collaborative culture that bears down on all the internal workings of departments.

The nature of quality in learning history was considered in Chapters 3 and 4. The prime imperative for history departments is to deliver a service that allows students, at all times, to achieve quality learning in the subject. This simple definition of quality in history provides the overarching basis for action by departments. This may be seen as a preferential as opposed to an objective notion of quality. In the manufacturing sector, quality is generally associated with the product being made. This can be measured and demonstrated in a tangible sense through, for example, sales figures, the reliability of the product and the nature of after-sale services. The nature of quality in history departments is not judged primarily in terms of its teaching but whether it enables students to achieve particular goals, (e.g. success as opposed to failure; GCSE and A level grades that allow progression; enjoyment) that are preferred to other goals.

This preferential view – particularly important for history departments that seek to improve the quality of the service they are providing – generates a triangular model of service quality (Morgan and Murgatroyd, 1994, pp.11–14).

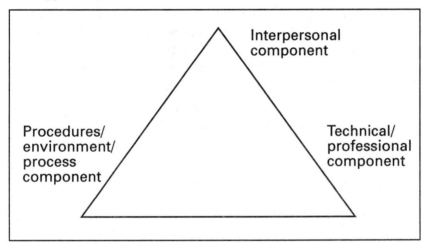

Figure 5.1 Triangular model of service quality

The relationship and balance between the three elements shown in Figure 5.1 are crucial and bear comparison with the notion of 'separation of powers' developed by Montesquieu (1748) and used by political and legal theorists. Montesquieu assumed a balance between the three 'powers' of legislature, executive and judiciary if the 'body politic' was to function efficiently and that any imbalance between the powers led to poor governance. The same principle applies to service quality. A history department places considerable emphasis on procedures and processes. The message students get from this is quite clear: 'You're a unit of service and we're all here to process you using our procedures'. Over-focusing on the interpersonal can be equally damaging: 'We're here to make history enjoyable for you and we'll try our best but we're not exactly sure what we're doing'. Too much emphasis on the professional and technical aspects results in students getting the following message: 'We're organised, know exactly what we're doing, but we're not really concerned with you as an individual. What matters are overall results.' The key to successful teaching and learning in history is to get the balance between these three powers right through a holistic approach to managing departments. We have already seen that emphasising the interpersonal leads to more effective student learning. Students certainly feel that the quality of the service provided is enhanced where teachers are willing to help students individually. They also place considerable emphasis on the technical and professional element, particularly where they feel that teachers know their subject well – a perception reinforced by the findings of Stanford University's 'Teacher Assessment Project' and 'Knowledge Growth in a Profession Project'. The remainder of the chapter considers the third element: the procedures/environment/process component.

Having a 'thing' about quality

The development of TQM is not something history departments can generally do in isolation. TQM is a strategic issue for schools as a whole and requires the production of medium and long-term organisation-wide plans. These itemise the quality scope of future strategy through a corporate vision statement (see Murgatroyd and Morgan, 1993, for the nature of corporate vision), goals, objectives and action plans that have an explicit quality orientation chosen to obtain the best competitive advantage within the particular market. History departments function within this holistic framework. However, departments can use the tools of TQM to alter radically the ways in which they operate even if schools as a whole do not go down this path. West-Burnham (1992, p.26) provides a useful summary of the key features of TQM and I intend to use these as a basis for discussing having 'a thing' about quality in managing history.

Quality defined by the customer, not the supplier

Students and parents are the primary customers of history departments. TQM has refined and extended the notion of the customer to include customers external to, and within, the organisation. Under TQM the critical question for each member of a history department is, 'Do I meet the needs of my customers or users?' The importance of this question may be obvious when dealing with students or parents. However, heads of history need to ask the same question about their subject teachers. History teachers can be seen as both customers and suppliers. Hence in TQM practice, the customer can also be a colleague in the department not just the student who is the receiver of the department's service.

History departments can establish clearly agreed routines that can be re-examined and reshaped in the light of the school's vision and strategy. As students progress through their history courses, on a sort of customer 'journey', they experience the history curriculum as a set of processes that provide varying degrees of certainty and unpredictability. This journey begins with their first history lesson and this, in many respects, sets a standard against which they judge their subsequent experiences. Beginning at a new school is often a traumatic experience for students. They have moved from the known to the unknown. It is likely that the secondary school will be bigger than their primary schools; there will be more activity and, particularly, more movement. This is confusing and can be frightening. They will not know all their fellow students or what is expected of them and they are very unlikely to know their teachers. History departments need to make this transition as smooth as possible so that students can go beyond their 'fears' and get on with the process of learning history. This means 'mapping' the journey from the point of view of the student: what does the student, as customer, need at this stage? Research on transfer from middle to upper schools, based on students' written evaluations four weeks into their courses, shows clearly that students have the following expectations from their first lesson in history (Brown, 1993):

- Expectations of the department and the class teacher need to be made explicit, particularly in relation to routines (when and where homework is to be handed in, for example).

- Students expect to be given outline information about what they will be doing during the year.

- Students, especially the more able, appear to welcome a brief synopsis mapping where Year 9 history fits into their possible progression routes 13–18.

Mapping processes is a valuable technique for understanding, examining and seeking to maximise the services provided by history departments. This is particularly the case when used in a team. Take, for example, the way a department prepares for an open evening. First, it is necessary to map in as much detail as possible the process for doing this: for example, who is responsible for what and when. Then each element of the process needs to be looked at in detail as a potential area for improvement: for example, can the department improve the quality of its displays? It is by improving the quality of the parts of a process that the process overall is improved. This means an audit of the process in terms of meeting customer needs: does the process allow potential customers to obtain a valid experience of history in the school? Finally, the department needs to establish 'quality benchmarks' against which the process can be reviewed: for example, asking customers to fill in a brief questionnaire and reaching a certain percentage of satisfied customers. Mapping is a demanding process for history departments, requiring a great deal of effort and focused work on details and minutiae. It is here that the most important gains in quality occur. By mapping student needs and expectations in a structured way and developing transfer procedures as a consequence it is possible that customer expectations can be fully met and even exceeded.

Nothing ever goes as smoothly as planned. TQM thinking suggests that the quality of a customer's experience of a service is strongly influenced by 'moments of truth' when the quality, or lack of quality, of the service or experience is very obvious to the student. These will affect the ways students think of and, what is more important, talk about the service. Take, for example, the reaction of a student who believes that she will be given individual help with a problem in understanding the causes of the First World War when the teacher with whom she has made an appointment to discuss the matter fails to turn up because he has forgotten. The issue here for the student is a sense of discrepancy between what she was led to expect and what she experienced in practice. The consequence will be a loss of trust by the student in the service ostensibly provided by the department. The aim for managers of history is to ensure that there is as little discrepancy as possible between student expectation and teacher response. So how can we minimise this discrepancy?

Moments of truth are important for departments. Murgatroyd and Morgan (1993, p.103) suggest three ways in which they have an impact on what departments do. Firstly, they provide insights into the expectations of students and parents about their role. Secondly, they give departments the chance to learn about improvement opportunities. Finally, they are moments for making change possible by quickly recognising that there are weaknesses in departmental processes and responding to them. This can enhance the standing of history in the eyes of the individual students or parents concerned. History departments cannot plan for all eventualities but by examining customer journeys carefully and seeking to identify moments of truth they can make a significant difference to the experience of students. When designing their range of learning services departments should seek to understand those services from the customer's point of view and then tailor their plans to fulfil customer expectations.

Measuring customer satisfaction is at the heart of TQM. This has a strong moral dimension. History departments do not merely obtain comments from students but they have an obligation to act on them. There is a parallel requirement on students to articulate their requirements and then to participate in monitoring and review. TQM is about effective collaboration between students and teachers so that students can demonstrate and develop quality in their learning.

Meeting stated needs, goals and standards

Central to TQM is the belief that identifying needs, stating aims and evaluating the quality of outcomes is achieved through improving the many processes that take place within history departments. Heads of history have to address the challenge posed by the question: 'How do we get all members of history departments to be committed to quality performance and continuous improvement in such a way that we can meet and exceed the expectations of those we are here to serve?' It is important to distinguish between 'outcome goals', like better examination results or a greater share of capitation, on which history departments tend to focus, and 'process goals' that are an explicit feature of TQM. It is possible to apply certain industrial process terms to the work of history departments in the following ways (Murgatroyd and Morgan,1993, pp.122–3):

- *Defections*. Reducing the loss of students to another department, for example, during the option process.

- *Zero Defects*. History teachers not making mistakes in the way processes and activities are conducted in their departments and ensuring that all benchmarked performance criteria are met.

- *Cycle time*. Departments work methodically to lessen the time it takes to complete any of their activities. Examples of this include reducing the time it takes at the beginning of a history lesson before effective learning takes place and the length of time it takes to teach a particular unit of study without loss of quality. If it were possible to reduce the amount of time before learning took place in a GCSE class by two minutes per lesson, this would amount to eight minutes per week or 560 minutes over a seventy week course: the equivalent of fourteen forty-minute lessons. The time made available could then be dedicated to additional learning activities .

- *On-time performance*. This is particularly important and is one area where customer judgement is especially vital. Teachers like to get history homework in on time and may use sanctions when this does not occur. Students do homework and like to get it back promptly and properly marked. Departments need to work towards a situation where all deadlines are met 100 per cent of the time for all.

- *Labour content of work.* History departments should be working to reduce the amounts of work individual teachers have to do for a given level of achievement while, at the same time, enhancing the individual's professional development. The time thus released can be allotted to essential tasks like preparing lessons and curriculum development or to developing expertise in new areas of pedagogy.

- *Plan to action time reduction.* Reducing the time taken between development, planning and testing of a new history course or activity and its full implementation.

- *Maximising customer satisfaction.* Increasing the level of satisfaction with the work of departments expressed by all customers, internal and external.

Goal setting is still in its infancy in most history departments yet it is central to TQM. Departments should be setting themselves outrageous goals, radical and massive leaps forward, but most goals are much smaller, allowing the maximising of improvements: remember the suggestion of chaos theory that small changes can have major consequences. Whatever goals are identified they need to be tied to the development of quality student learning in specific and measurable ways.

History departments also have to take account of the 'value-added' nature of their activities. This idea is particularly valuable when considering those activities that detract from value by adding costs (Morgan and Murgatroyd, 1994, pp.30–2). Are the processes used by departments as efficient as they can be? For example, a newly introduced system for dealing with students identified several process steps necessary for dealing with problems. This built on an already existing system by extending the number of steps available before students were given after-school detentions. Was it an improvement on the existing system? In value-added terms it could only be seen in this light if it reduced costs. Many processes have too many steps that add little or no value to their outcomes. The same criteria can be applied to preparation time for developing new initiatives. A newly planned Era of the Second World War unit required eight one-hour planning meetings of five teachers (forty person-hours). Could this have been reduced? Poor record-keeping causes delays in making decisions and reduces effectiveness. The point of these examples is to show that non-value-adding activities take valuable time, energy and resources away from the primary imperative of delivering quality student learning. Redesigned systems can eliminate these sources of value-losing activity and result in an improvement in the perceived quality of the service with lower operating costs.

Continuous improvement by prevention, not detection

Deming (1988) argues that 85 per cent of production faults are the responsibility of management not employees. Inspection will not resolve this problem because it occurs afterwards and is often ineffective and costly. He suggests an emphasis on precision, performance and attention to customers' needs, using statistical methods as a way of achieving 'constancy of purpose'. What history departments must do is to ensure quality by preventing errors from occurring rather than simply by detecting them later. Suppose a meeting is set up to discuss problems students are having with the Year 7 Medieval Realms unit and the time of the meeting is communicated poorly to the relevant staff by the head of history. Three staff turn up and have to wait for the others not to arrive; the result is a re-scheduled meeting, frustration for staff with the head of department and delays in making what could be crucial decisions about individual student learning. This may seem to be a comparatively minor issue but the cost implications for departments are significant. Some writers have suggested that they amount to as much as 40 per cent of total costs.

Senior management led but a shared responsibility

Quality is driven by senior managers but is an equal responsibility of all those involved in any process. The organisational culture outlined in previous chapters is radically different from traditional management models and certainly these have to alter to accommodate TQM. History departments that have adopted TQM have developed a collaborative culture in which (Morgan and Murgatroyd, 1994, p.16):

- Innovation is highly valued.

- Status is secondary to performance and contribution.

- Leadership is a consequence of action, not position.

- Rewards are shared through the work of teams.

- Development, learning and training are recognised as critical means of sustaining quality.

- Empowerment to achieve challenging goals supported by continued development and successes provide a climate for self-motivation.

The senior manager may be the driving force behind strategic change but it is within departments that heads of history maximise the power of teachers nearest to the students. This gives classroom teachers ownership of changes and an important stake in successfully making those changes that improve quality in learning. Project teams within history departments can perhaps best be seen as a network of units free to act while retaining their links with each other, with senior managers shaping overall direction.

Statistical measurement and monitoring

Quality is measured by statistical methods. At the core of TQM is the notion that every task is a process that needs to be managed and its performance monitored. Statistical Process Control (SPC) is therefore a key concept in TQM. SPC methods provide objective means of controlling quality using two kinds of data:

- *Variable data.* This includes everything that varies in measurable terms such as the amounts of time individual history teachers take to teach a unit of work or the time students take to understand a new idea or the amount of time spent on individual interviews at parents' evenings.

- *Attribute or countable data.*

SPC aims to discourage focus on impressionistic individual pieces of data and concentrates systematically on the process as a whole. It is also a means of making decisions about the quality of particular tasks as a result of data collection and analysis.

SPC lets history departments produce *control charts* and undertake *cost-benefit analysis*. Control charts allow teachers to determine whether something is or is not in control. This means measuring acceptable ranges of behaviour within a system – upper and lower limits – and then looking at behaviour that falls in and out of these ranges. Take as an example detentions given by members of a department. These could be calculated over time and by teacher, and by detentions for lack of homework, lack of work in class and unacceptable behaviour. The mean could then be calculated for each teacher. Looking at upper and lower limits is more valuable for determining whether an individual history teacher has problems compared to the rest of the department and in what particular areas (see Oakland, 1986, for an accessible approach to this subject).

Cost-benefit analysis applies to capital investment like books and computer software but it also applies to curriculum planning, development and implementation. It looks systematically at the benefits that are derived from decisions to undertake particular tasks (Oakland, 1989). What value is added as a result of one decision rather than another? A history department is considering changing to a new GCSE syllabus. Numbers opting for history have fallen by a quarter in the last three years as a result of competition from geography. The question the department has to consider is whether to change (buy) or to resist change (don't buy). It has to consider the probable consequences of the costs involved and the benefits that may accrue. This can be shown in the form of a decision tree as in Figure 5.2.

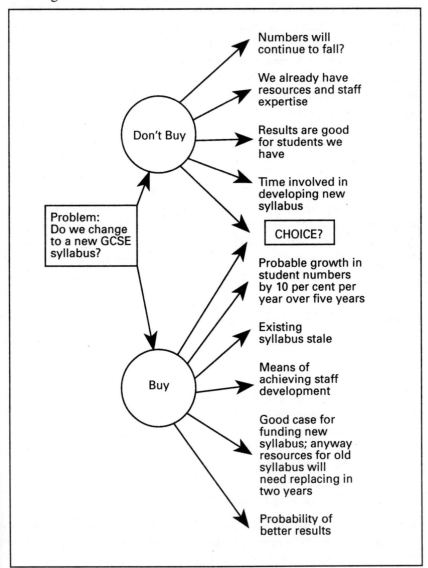

Figure 5.2 Cost-benefit decision tree

Measuring quality means that history departments have to develop *benchmarks* against which judgements can be made. In simple terms this means that they measure their products, services and practices against their competition. The aim is to improve the quality of performance so that it approximates to the 'best in its class'. National league tables, for all their defects, provide some basis for this competitive benchmarking. Internal benchmarking, where comparisons are made between similar processes performed by different teachers, is perhaps of greater value in improving the quality of history departments. Why do some history teachers take longer to teach a particular unit of work than others but with the same levels of learning outcomes? Departments can develop, as a result of statistical analysis, their own *service standard*. This recognises that teaching and learning history are customer-driven and that there are agreed levels of performance that are observable, attainable, measurable and desirable.

Teamwork

Quality has to pervade human relationships in the work place; teams are the most powerful agent for managing quality. TQM sees teams as fundamental to a commitment to learning and to changes for improving quality. We have already seen that managing history departments as learning organisations through project teams is essential if there is to be a search for continuous improvement. Without this, there is a danger that existing processes will simply be replicated uncritically and significant improvements in quality learning not achieved. The main limitation on the effective running of teams is 'balkanisation', a compartmentalisation of effort where history departments are working for themselves and do not recognise the needs of other departments or schools as a whole. TQM maintains that departments in schools have both joint and separate interests and that there is interdependence and autonomy. Heads of history as team leaders have a central role to play in this situation with responsibility for improving quality among their teachers but also recognising the place of history within the overall curriculum. Teams empower teachers in ways that traditional methods of management failed to do.

Education, training and personal growth

Quality can only be achieved by a valued work force, and TQM assumes a learning organisation in which staff development is an essential feature. Everyone is trained for quality, and investment in training – whether of time or money – is central to improving the overall quality of history departments. Establishing priorities is important for heads of history when determining staff development and the critical questions always have to be: 'What value in improving the quality of student learning within the department can be achieved by a teacher attending this course? In what ways will attending this course make the teacher a more valuable member of the departmental team?' Cost-effectiveness and personal development are the keys.

Intrinsic quality

Quality has to be the criterion for reviewing every decision, every action and every process. Quality is the driving-force behind each decision history departments make. Quality is, however, a process of continuous improvement that is the responsibility of everyone in the department. It is a philosophy for action, of anticipation and planning, of continuous review and enterprise driven by goals and values. It seeks to add value to existing services by placing the customer first.

Having a 'thing' about quality is an essential prerequisite for a successful department that is customer-driven. It leads to efficiency and effectiveness and to proactivity. TQM provides heads of history with the necessary management tools for making their departments more effective as teams, as learning organisations and as deliverers of services.

Projecting quality

Project management is about getting things done by making things happen. It involves determining what is to be done, how, when, where, by whom and at what cost. It is fundamentally about risk. Any project has risks associated with it. Managing projects involves spotting the risks and acting to reduce them. A managed project is one where events are not simply left to chance. Instead they are planned, organised and arranged into sequences with anticipated duration, costs and consequences. Quality learning in history does not materialise spontaneously, or at least not very often.

If you ask a head of history if he intends to improve the quality of his students' learning, he'll certainly say yes. Then ask him how? If he doesn't know he probably won't succeed. Things are rarely achieved by mere chance. Getting them done requires planning, pushing things in the direction of the plan, setting deadline dates and checking that the steps along the way are on track. There are several ways of categorising the main steps in project planning. TQM suggests that three are of particular importance: *planning, communicating* and *controlling*. Planning leads to the development of a plan. This must be communicated to others so they know what has been planned. Once agreed and in progress, the project must be controlled through a monitoring process. Variance will inevitably creep in, things slip and are done late. The plan has to be revisited, the good (or bad) news communicated and the (perhaps revised) plan then placed back on the control cycle.

Planning within the framework of collaborative cultures is a central feature of TQM. Heads of history need to be clear what sort of plans they are developing with their teams. Crisis management is a not uncommon feature of history departments – what has been called 'adhocracy'. Departments lurch from one crisis to the next with planning priorities, if they can be called that, determined by what pressing problem needs to be resolved at that moment. If there is no organisational development plan within a department this is likely to be the approach adopted. This is not to decry crisis management unduly; it is necessary if departments are to respond flexibly to particular situations, but, if it constitutes the only method of departmental planning it is unlikely to provide a basis for effective quality development in anything, let alone student learning.

Davies and Ellison (1992) suggest that there are three levels of planning within schools:

1. *Strategic planning,* largely by governors and heads. This is concerned with broad policies and goals on a one- to three-year basis. It relates the organisation to its environment, and predicts the effects of changes on that environment, like rising or falling student numbers.

2. *Tactical planning* is more routine and takes place within the guidelines of the strategic plan. It is the concern of headteachers, senior staff and middle management. It provides the framework of activity that allows the strategic plan to be met, emphasising the specific objectives of particular activities like curriculum development and timetabling.

3. *Operational planning* emphasises the day-to-day implementation of particular activities and is the concern of all teachers.

These three types of planning undoubtedly do have a whole-school orientation but, I suggest, they are equally applicable to history departments if they are to be TQM organisations.

Without a focus on strategic, tactical and operational planning history departments will adopt a short-term emphasis to their planning. Heads of history have become accustomed to tactical planning over the last ten years in producing their annual departmental development plans. These are increasingly seen as essential: externally they are used by OFSTED as one of its sources of quality; internally they are an indispensable part of the budgetary arguments heads of history put forward when seeking funding for resourcing curriculum development. They require heads of history to lay down priorities and procedures to monitor how the plan is being achieved. The problem with this approach is that it encourages a 'yearly mentality', a cyclical pattern of objectives and priorities which tends to reinforce the *status quo* or forces drastic but temporary measures on departments. Without strategic planning, even when schools build in longer-term aims, departmental plans can become paper exercises more concerned with enhancing capitation than effecting long-term strategies for achieving improvements in student learning.

If tactical planning leads to 'short-termism' then strategic planning can become remote from the operational management of departments. There is a long-held belief in schools that planning and goal-setting is something done by senior and middle managers and that teachers get on with the job of teaching in the classroom. How many times have heads of history heard their colleagues say that the plan looks good on paper but how will it be transferred to the classroom? Sound strategic planning should focus on process goals that affect all aspects of departmental activity and the daily activities of history teachers. The critical question history teachers need to ask is: 'How does strategic planning translate into daily events and what effect does it have on student learning?'

There are several problems history departments have to face when developing plans at whatever level. Firstly, TQM maintains that plans must be measurable. This means that identified goals should be capable of being quantified easily. It is essential to avoid difficult-to-measure goals. An example that often finds its way into the aims of history departments is: making students more tolerant of others as a result of learning history. What does this mean in practice and how can we measure it? Alternatively, history departments can set perfectly measurable goals but then not measure them. This undermines the whole notion of TQM because no systematic attempt is made to learn from performance and the annual cycle of departmental planning is reinforced. The object of TQM is to improve quality year-on-year and without effective measurement the potential of departments for organisational learning and development is diminished. Secondly, TQM is about action, about implementing agreed goals for improvement. This means that goals need to be written clearly so that there is minimal ambiguity. Failure to do this will result in goals either being ignored or interpreted differently across departments. The result is confusion and the potential for interpretative conflict. Thirdly, TQM is about implementing plans. Consequently plans need to be realistic. As head of history I might want to change all my syllabuses this year but will I get the necessary resources to do so? Probably not. So why is this a goal in my annual plan? It may look good on paper and make members of my department feel good about what we're doing. In practice, however, it is not going to happen, or at least not how we've planned. Fourthly, it does not matter how good the planning is if there is no effective communication. Finally, planning can become part of a political game within departments and thus divorced from the prime imperative of ensuring effective quality learning. Collaborative cultures ensure that there is alignment with everyone involved and commitment with everyone working to the agreed goals. Playing politics is divisive and usually guarantees that plans will not be implemented effectively, if at all. How does TQM assist history departments to plan effectively for improvement?

TQM helps teams of history teachers to think more critically about the problems they face and engage with daily. It is about ensuring that students learn history effectively. Although considerable emphasis has been placed upon the need for measurement this is not an end in itself but an aid to understanding and decision-making. TQM is about learning to think about quality and, as a result, act to achieve quality. A history department has identified improving the quality of teaching for GCSE classes as one of its goals for the next year. How does TQM help? Murgatroyd and Morgan (1993) suggest a six stage approach:

1. *The department needs to collect basic information*. This data-collection stage is of fundamental importance since it provides an actual, as opposed to a supposed, basis on which to build. The team needs to look at results of teaching, teaching strategies employed, the syllabuses taught and so on. This will make the nature of the problem clear and allow clear goals to be established that allow action to occur.

2. *Ideas then need to be converted into measures*. Measurable goals need to be established. They may be realistic or outrageous or a combination of the two. A realistic goal could be that all teachers will employ at least two different teaching approaches in each lesson while an outrageous goal could be that teachers will be paired and will observe each other's lessons on a weekly basis. Securing wide support for goals is essential and here a collaborative culture within the department is a considerable advantage.

3. *Analysing processes* is the next stage when the team uses process mapping and other tools to understand the processes they have developed.

4. *Designed improved processes*. Analysis of processes is followed by seeking to improve them.

5. *Establish standards.* Targets need to be established for the work and a time schedule built into this. The history department might decide that by the end of the Autumn term it will reach stage 2 of the process and by Easter stage 4.

6. *Managing performance.* Levels of performance need to be considered against the standards the team established for itself. What has it achieved? Has teaching GCSE improved and in what ways? Is there any evidence of failure? What is it and why did it occur? This process of monitoring performance is essential if the project is to be maintained and teaching standards to be continuously improved.

This is a cyclical process that rolls forward, a situation where the process begins again once stage 6 has been reached. This is planning for action and improvement and for quality student learning in history.

TQM is about effective communication within history departments, within teams and between students and teachers. It is about partnership. What must history teachers do to deliver TQM? Equally, what must students do to deliver total quality in learning to their teachers? There must be a mutual commitment to quality leading to increased motivation and continuous improvement. Quality learning is a consequence of dialogue through which effective and cost effective change can be achieved. Customers and suppliers are two sides of the same coin. This cliché is at the heart of TQM.

Quality, collaboration and the learning organisation

Most history teachers would accept that the goal of achieving quality student learning is both worthwhile and necessary. Yet many challenge the TQM method of achieving this. Morgan and Murgatroyd (1994, pp.98–104) suggest that this challenge comes from six sources:

1. *A rejection of industrial models and language: an anti-management tendency.* History teachers are caring people who want the best for their students. They, however, recognise that there are a range of factors that militate against individual students achieving success and although they try to mitigate these factors there are occasions when there is little they can do positively about them. The best they can do is to provide students with experiences and values that may well have nothing to do with success in the world beyond school. Why, they argue, should we prepare students for the vagaries of the outside world by pushing economic values grounded in the market and by achieving levels of

success that most students will not be able to replicate outside. This view is based on a false perception of the nature of TQM as being about preparing students for work. History departments that hold this view are likely to take a professional perception of their role, defining goals *for* students rather than allowing them to define their own goals and then deliver quality learning.

2. *There is a tradition of individual rather than collective responsibility for quality.* History teachers are individuals with individual responsibility for ensuring that *their* students learn effectively. This individual autonomy is reflected in the insulated perceptions they have of *their* classrooms. TQM seeks to develop department-wide dimensions of quality requiring a collaborative approach to teaching and learning. This poses a challenge to the sanctity of the classroom.

3. *TQM is about the organisational context of the school rather than the classroom.* While history departments may well accept that there is a possibility of improving its administration and procedures, there is considerable scepticism about subjecting the complex processes of teaching and learning to scrutiny or technical analysis. This view is grounded in a hierarchical view of management that, roughly stated, maintains that 'managers manage and teachers teach'. There tends to be an absence of systematic evaluation or only evaluation based upon impressions rather than hard data. This seems to neglect the primary aim of history departments, which is the improvement of the quality of student learning, and makes an unjustifiable division between the process of management and the process of teaching and learning history. It presumes that TQM provides no insight or means of analysing what is going on in the classroom.

4. *There is a widespread belief that performance achievement is the consequence of inputs.* Students achieve high quality learning in history, it is argued, because of key input factors like class size, levels of resourcing or students' intrinsic abilities. How many times have heads of history heard their colleagues say that if only they had smaller classes then the results would be better? What evidence there is on school effectiveness suggests that there is no simple correlation between quality and input factors. How can students in one school with limited resources do better than a neighbouring school with smaller class sizes and a 'better' intake of students? Clearly input factors are not the reason.

5. *We are doing very well as we are.* Your department has excellent results in relation to your competitors and your students and parents are quite happy with the service being provided. Complacency rules. Just

because a department is doing well does not mean that the local 'marketplace' will not change or that it cannot do better and achieve higher levels of quality and customer approval. TQM provides, through the notion of continuous improvement, an effective and critical process for achieving this.

6. *There is a tradition of centralised decision-making in history departments.* Heads of history are paid to run their departments and to make the decisions. They may operate through a system of contrived collaboration but ultimately decision-making is top-down. TQM empowers staff and students, encouraging individual initiative, higher levels of effective communication and the continuous improvement of quality. Management by control is replaced by facilitative leadership in which heads of departments are team leaders or process managers.

The effective implementation of TQM means that these cultural challenges have to be overcome. It represents a paradigm shift from traditional management to a whole new way of managing by history departments.

Senge (1990, p.313) argues that

Human beings learn best through firsthand experience. We learn to walk, to ride a bicycle, drive an automobile, and play the piano by trial and error: we act, observe the consequences of our action and adjust. But 'learning by doing' only works so long as the feedback from our actions is rapid and unambiguous...we learn best from experience, but we never experience the consequences of our most important decisions. How, then, can we learn?

The history department as a learning organisation is one where people, whether teachers or students, continually expand their capacities to create the results they truly desire, where new and expansive patterns of thinking are nurtured, where collective aspiration is set free and where people are continually learning how to learn together (Senge, 1990, p.3). TQM means quality learning, collaboration and history departments as learning organisations. It empowers teachers and students and liberates departmental management from the contrived collaboration and control that characterises traditional methods of managing. It places the customer to the fore and recognises that continuous improvement in services for the consumer is the standard against which the processes of teaching and learning can be judged. If it doesn't result in quality student learning, then don't do it.

CHAPTER 6

Appraising Performance

> In fact, the subtle dynamics of WonderTech confirm an intuition of many experienced managers: that it is vital to hold to critical performance standards 'through thick and thin' and to do whatever it takes to meet those standards. The standards that are most important are those that matter the most to the customer...product quality, delivery service, service reliability and quality, and friendliness and concern of service personnel.
>
> Senge (1990, p.123)

It's the day A level history results are published. There's the usual flutter in the morning newspapers. Numbers taking A level have increased and the percentage passing or getting grades A to C is better than last year. The usual criticism that A level is getting easier and the usual denials from the examination boards that this is the case. Tearful students. It doesn't seem to matter whether they've got the grades they need or have to go through the lottery of 'clearing'. Pats on the back from headteachers for those history departments with good grades and the obligatory, 'well, we knew this year's students were weaker and next year's will be better', for those that haven't. The head of history is pleased. The results are good, a marked improvement on last year's poor showing. The customers are happy. A good performance all round, from her teachers and students. A levels or GCSEs or any form of testing certainly provide an important snapshot of quality learning and furnish valuable benchmarks against which to judge the effectiveness of departments. But are these external judgements enough? I think not. What applies to WonderTech should apply to history departments.

This chapter considers two central issues in appraising the performance of history departments. Firstly, it asks how teachers can evaluate student learning to ensure that quality is continuously improved. This means looking at how the quality of the product delivered by departments is evaluated and how it can be improved. Secondly, we need to look at how departments appraise the means by which teachers deliver a quality service. This is considered in two respects: the appraisal of individual teachers and departmental inspection through the medium of OFSTED.

Evaluating student learning

At a simple level, evaluation means placing a value on things. A more exhaustive definition is, however, provided by Borich and Jemelka (1982):

> ...the primary purpose of evaluation has been to provide decision-makers with information about the effectiveness of some programme, product or procedure...Despite differences in the conceptual frameworks used by practitioners there has been basic agreement about the decision-making role of evaluation.

The information that provides the basis for decision-making may either be quantitative, involving measurement, or qualitative, meaning that value-judgements are at the heart of decisions. It is the systematic nature of evaluating learning in history that provides the basis for the accountability of students and history teachers (Becher and Maclure, 1987; Aspinwall, 1992).

The evaluation of student learning is something that history teachers and, increasingly, students do, formally or informally, all the time (see Cangelosi, 1991). This is often uncomplicated. A history teacher observes that, during a lesson on The Black Death, the oral contribution from a particular Year 7 student is far more articulate than usual, demonstrating a sound understanding of the issues raised by the topic. The teacher comments positively to the student. Other students, after the lesson, remark on the teacher's comment. Well-answered homework is rewarded with formal commendations and positive teacher observations. Evaluation, in this sense, is essentially *diagnostic* or *formative*, concerned with identifying and praising successful learning while identifying weakness in understanding or application that may stand in the way of quality learning. Evaluation may also be *summative,* appraising the overall effectiveness of student learning over a longer time. Irrespective of the form student evaluation takes its primary aim is to help students demonstrate and develop their grasp of history, whether methodological or contextual, through a collaborative framework of teaching and learning.

The major difficulty history teachers have with this view of evaluation is that, as Goddard and Leask (1992, p.155) suggest, 'Working collaboratively to solve a problem is not the hallmark of the current political approach.' Evaluating students has become politicised, particularly in 'league tables', and linked to how effectively teachers do their job. This is a crude instrument which can be demotivating for teachers and students and will almost certainly not lead to the goal of improved quality of learning unless linked to more sophisticated forms of assessment and evaluation.

Principles for evaluating learning in history

History teachers first have to be clear about the basis for their evaluation of learning. Goddard and Leask (1992, pp.159–60) suggest several principles as together forming an initial step towards securing reliable and valid evaluation procedures within institutions. These have been adapted to provide a set of dependable and valid procedures grounded in developing quality learning through TQM.

Evaluation as part of a broader process

Evaluation must be part of a broader process of improvement embracing all features of departmental development. Evaluation is an explicit feature of TQM. Its principles and practices are integrated into the every-day working approach of history departments. The professional operation of teachers and students is constantly evaluated as a central part of the improvement of the quality of their work. In this sense evaluation is seen *as* improvement.

Links with action plans

Judgements and reporting are related to an agreed action plan. Evaluation cannot take place in isolation from what students have negotiated and agreed in their action plans for improved learning in history. Without this process of negotiation and agreement any judgement or reporting by teachers will lack validity. Action planning, linked to the process of continuous improvement in learning, reinforces the collaborative nature of learning history and allows appropriate judgements to be drawn that can then be reported internally and externally.

Shared responsibility for improvement

All parties to the services provided by history departments have a shared responsibility to maintain and improve the quality of their work. Evaluation is not unidimensional. It is not something that teachers alone do. Collaborative learning demands a collaborative approach to evaluation with students and teachers involved together in establishing a clear evaluative framework within which students' achievements in learning can be celebrated.

Agreed ethical and technical procedures

The collection and presentation of evidence, the establishment of criteria, the making of judgements and reporting are separate though interrelated parts of the overall process and should be subject to agreed ethical and technical procedures. Evaluation of students should develop from the collection of evidence rather than from subjective impressions. This will provide a clear basis on which to make judgements and should ensure that what is reported has validity (see Adelman, 1984, on important ethical questions).

Fit for the purpose

The form of evaluation should be related to its purpose. The primary purpose of any evaluation should be to improve student learning. Teachers first need to recognise and value what is already taking place. This provides a diagnostic benchmark of student achievement, a snapshot of where they are now in their understanding of history. Reliable information about the strengths and weaknesses of students needs to be collected, thus enabling the most effective next steps to be identified. Information provided at transfer from primary or middle schools is of particular value for history teachers, another argument for the value of effective inter-school liaison. Establishing a common task to be taken by all students before transfer and moderated by all the schools concerned is particularly valuable in establishing a clear evaluation of student learning. Failing this, some history departments 'test' students as soon as they transfer.

The primary purpose of evaluation then becomes formative building on the base already identified. Evaluation *for* improvement in student learning is the major goal. This will take various forms. There will be *quality control* as a means of policing learning with appropriate help for those students having problems, *quality assurance* concerned with the identification and achievement of quality learning and *quality development* that identifies an improvement in the established standards of learning history. A student transferred to his secondary school with an overall attainment level of 2. This level was borne out by his school's internal diagnostic tests in the first month of his Year 7 course. Discussions with the student resulted in an agreed action plan to improve to level 3 by the end of the year. Quality control was applied when his level of work failed to reach the agreed standards. For example, two particularly poor pieces of homework were followed by an interview with the student to ascertain whether there was a problem in understanding a particular topic and action was taken to mitigate his difficulties. The development in the quality of his learning was recorded weekly with three commendations given for particularly good pieces of work. At the end of the year he had achieved level 3, reaching an assured level of achievement. A similar process was used with him throughout the five years he studied history (leading to a grade B at GCSE) using a combination of collaborative action planning, control and rewards for achievement. In this way evaluation contributed directly to the achievement and maintenance of quality learning.

Open and explicit

The procedures should be open and explicit and laid down in such a way that they command the respect and confidence of all those who have a legitimate interest in the service. It is not possible to improve student learning without checking and analysing their strengths and weaknesses. Students need to feel confident that evaluation is not just something done to them by teachers but something in which they have a recognised stake. If they do not, it is highly likely that evaluation will not lead to improved learning in history and will be viewed entirely as a matter of quality control. Evaluating students in history is a process that should be shared with teachers and must be open. This does not mean that every piece of evaluation should be available to absolutely everyone. It is unlikely that teachers would expose their evaluation of students to others if this meant exposing them to ridicule. However, there is a strong case for openness when students have achieved their goals. Recognising that evaluation has different levels and that different actions are appropriate to different situations is important.

Effectiveness

The system shall be effective. There is no point history departments developing systems of evaluation that are ineffective and do not contribute to the decision-making process for teachers and students. Evaluation must be worthwhile and credible for teachers and students, its purposes clear and its potential value to students explicit. The outcomes of evaluation must be valuable for all parties concerned, its judgements must have validity by being based on verifiable evidence and the process must be viable and sustainable by being cost-effective in terms of time and resources. Students, and teachers, respond best to an evaluation system that is short and simple.

In evaluation the process is as important as the product (see Hopkins,

1989, especially pp.97–115). *How* things are done is often at least as important as *what* is done. Successful evaluation of learning in history is based upon judging whether students have achieved the goals agreed in their action plans. If they have, then evaluation provides a means for moving forward to more outrageous goals. If not, teachers and students have to ask why goals have not been achieved and what actions are now necessary to carry intentions into concrete quality action.

Evaluation as learning in history

Improving student learning in history is a process of change. Student confidence is a fundamental element of this process, of which an essential part is establishing a clear pedagogical and procedural basis for evaluation. History departments operate within a whole-school policy of evaluation and reporting. This will be laid down in the forward plan each year. It is this public and external dimension of profiling, examinations, parents evenings and reporting that forms the framework on which departments build their own collaborative system for evaluating student achievement.

For evaluation to be effective the first thing students need is information about the history courses they are following and what is expected of them by their teachers. Reproducing the syllabus may be adequate for GCSE and A level but a simplified version is necessary for Years 7 to 9. This has two advantages. Firstly, it demands that teachers plan their courses for their teaching groups taking account of the different abilities of students. Secondly, it provides students with a clear summary of the aims and content of the course. Important dates, like end-of-module tests, profiling dates and examinations, can be included in the course framework, enabling students to plan their time more effectively. My evaluation of sixty Year 9 and 11 students suggests that they valued this approach: 'It allowed me to plan out my time during the course. If only other subject teachers had done the same thing I think I would have been able to learn better.' (Year 11 student); 'The year plan gave me confidence and a clear idea of when I had to do things by.' (Year 11 student) 'It showed that the teacher was organised and knew what she was doing. It made me feel more confident about my work.' (Year 9 student).

A criticism that has been made is that this approach is too regimented and leaves no flexibility for the unpredictable. This is certainly true if history teachers feel bound to follow their plans slavishly. Flexibility of approach is essential and this can be achieved by leaving time available each term to allow topics to overrun if students are having difficulties with understanding or if they generate particular interest that teachers wish to follow up.

Once students know the extent of their courses it is possible to build in the process of evaluation. There are four basic stages to this process.

1. The identification of areas in need of improvement;
2. The setting of goals related to these areas;
3. The development of strategies for implementing these goals;
4. The evaluation of the stated goals against performance.

This process is easily understandable by teachers and students and results in improved achievement in history.

A collaborative approach to learning history often falls down at the first stage when teachers alone determine the areas in need of improvement. There may be a certain logic in this. Teachers have an experience of learning that students lack and will see the broader picture especially as they will have access to diagnostic information about students. There is, however, a very strong case for a twin-track approach at this stage with both teachers and students identifying learning needs. Self-evaluation by students – 'where I think I am now' – is a motivating force especially when it forms the basis of establishing goals for improved learning. This will give students confidence that their view will be listened to and gives them an explicit stake in the whole process. They no longer see evaluation as something that is done to them.

Setting goals, as we have already seen in Chapter 3, is the central part of the whole process and, for students, the most difficult. Student comments make this clear:

> Turning I want to get better marks on source questions into a goal is hard. What do I want to actually do? At present I get seven out of ten and I want to increase this to eight or nine but how? I'm good at getting factual information out of sources, I can say whether they're biased or not but I'm no good at dealing with opinions... (Student: Year 10)

> I can't write essays or at least I don't get very good marks. I want to get better marks. (Student: Year 11)

Students need to be helped to identify what they can do in a particular area of history and where it is possible for them to make improvements. These goals have to be specific. General goals, like 'I want to do better in history', are of little real value. Improvements in learning will occur as a result of small-scale developments in specific problem areas and do have a significant impact on the overall quality of learning. Some students can convert 'problems' into goals easily and all teachers need to do is to check these on their action plans. Others need more detailed help and this means interviewing students to discuss and formulate their goals. The age of particular students seems not to play a major role in their ability to formulate goals: sixth-form students are just as likely to have problems as Year 7 students. Developing student confidence in identifying goals for improvement is accompanied by a reduced need for direct teacher input.

Once students have identified their goals these become non-negotiable until the next round in the evaluation process. Evaluation will become untenable if students and teachers can change its parameters at will. The question teachers and students have to address now is: how can we translate goals into effective strategies for improved learning? It is easy for teachers at this stage to instruct students that they need to do X, Y and Z to carry out their goals. This gives teachers control but effectively emasculates students. Teachers are facilitators working with students to allow them to reach their specific goals. This stage of the process has four features:

1. *Establishing flexible planning approaches.* Students need to adopt a flexible and realistic approach to their planning. There is no point in students saying they intend to do something if it is unrealistic. For example, a planning strategy that stated that a student intended to do two hours history work per night at home would be untenable given the demands on that student's time from other subjects.

2. *Establishing clear deadlines.* This may seem to contradict the flexible approach advocated above. In fact it is an essential part of it. Deadlines are related to the process of improved learning but they must be re-negotiable allowing students to modify their planning when circumstances arise within history or more likely outside that they could not have predicted.

3. *Identifying areas where students need specific teacher help.* This may mean negotiating time with teachers outside lesson time when specific problems can be examined and assistance given.

4. *Establishing monitoring procedures.* These allow students and teachers to see whether goals are being developed and reached. Again this makes the case for flexibility of planning.

A Year 8 student identified that she would improve her ability to write more detailed answers to questions on the causes of events as one of her goals for the second half of the Autumn term. She had looked at her responses to questions for the first half of term and found that they averaged thirty words in length, giving her little space to extend her understanding of causation. She discussed the reasons for this with her teacher and identified two particular difficulties: she had problems distinguishing between short- and long-term causes and she had difficulty expressing her ideas on causes

120

at length. Both the teacher and student recognised that there were specific history problems and more general problems of expression in writing. It was agreed that her teacher would give the student three additional sessions at lunchtime specifically dealing with causation and that he would approach the English department to obtain more information about her writing difficulties. The student agreed that she would attend the sessions and would seek to double the length of her answers by the end of term. These became part of her planning strategy. She also agreed that she would gradually increase the amount she wrote over the next seven weeks: forty words by the end of a fortnight; fifty words by the end of a month; a process both she and her teacher would monitor. At the end of term she agreed to have a further meeting with her teacher so that her improvement in learning could be fully evaluated.

The final stage of the process is the evaluation of performance when teacher and student examine goals against achievement. This may be done formally through specific testing but self-evaluation may be the basis for evaluation. Both teachers and students are accountable at this stage. Students have to demonstrate their achievement and explain if they have not achieved their agreed goals. This then forms the basis for the next round of goal-setting, action-planning and evaluation.

This approach to evaluation as an integral part of learning history is effective. Work with students over the past five years shows clearly that where they are involved in identifying and setting goals and in planning strategies for implementing those goals there is a sustained improvement in the quality of their learning. It gives students the confidence to recognise the difficulties that prevent them achieving effective learning and establishes a collaborative and symbiotic relationship between teachers and their students in which respective roles and responsibilities are more clearly defined. Teachers and students adopt a reflective approach to learning but one grounded in the improvement of practice (James, 1989). Evaluation is no longer separate from learning in history. It has become the learning process.

Evaluating teachers' performance

Goddard and Leask (1992, p.157) suggest that 'The delivery of high-quality learning and subsequent teaching must be the subject of increasing professional examination...Teachers are being asked to fly to the moon with the research and development knowledge of the Napoleonic era.'

Appraisal and inspection are now seen, by government at least, as central to the process of improving student learning in history at both the individual and departmental levels. Neither can be effective without the other. Appraisal develops the individual teacher. Inspection provides an assessment, albeit something of a snapshot, of departmental and individual teacher development. The problem with both appraisal and inspection is that they may not increase the insight and understanding that lie at the heart of change and the improvement of quality learning. Inspection, particularly, is frequently perceived as threatening, as a means of identifying what needs to be improved and as something separate from the overall improvement of history departments. Appraisal is perceived as the first step towards performance-related pay. What their introduction has done is to raise the profile of notions of teacher accountability. Bush (1980) distinguished three types of accountability:

1. Moral accountability or being answerable to customers (students and parents);

2. Professional accountability or being responsible to oneself and colleagues;

3. Contractual accountability or being accountable to one's employers.

There is a constant tension between the three. For example, a Year 10 student goes to the head of history to complain about the quality of teaching by her GCSE teacher. The head of department is torn between being answerable to the student for the quality of her learning and her professional responsibilities for the effectiveness and responsiveness of the service being delivered by her department. Moral accountability is perhaps the strongest of the three. Teachers are certainly concerned for *their* students and a collaborative approach to learning increases that sense of responsibility. Professional accountability is perhaps the weakest of the three though its contribution to improved quality in learning is seminal. The move towards what is seen as a coercive contractual approach to accountability in the prescriptive nature of the National Curriculum, league tables, teacher appraisal and the redefined role of national inspection through OFSTED has sharpened the tension between the three accountabilities (Stake, 1989).

The effectiveness of appraisal and inspection is a matter of considerable debate. Early results from the Leverhulme Appraisal Project (Wragg, 1994, and the fuller account to be published in 1995) suggest that its impact on subsequent classroom practice varies considerably. Although 69 per cent of the sample of 1,000 teachers felt appraisal had been of benefit to them, mainly boosting confidence and self-awareness, only a disappointing 49 per cent of the sample said it did lead to a change in classroom practice. Student confidence and quality learning in history are more likely to be achieved when the relationship between the different forms of accountability is less starkly politicised. What is needed is a proper balance between the three. Goddard and Leask (1992) suggest that contractual accountability is the safety net, professional accountability provides an infrastructure of specialist responsibilities and that moral accountability is the driving force. Certainly this model of accountability is less threatening to history teachers since it places successful student learning in the forefront of departmental and individual teacher evaluation and improvement. The accountability of teachers is, in the same way as the evaluation of student learning, a continuous process rather than something that occurs when teachers are appraised or departments inspected. The management techniques outlined earlier in the book should mean that teacher evaluation is approached in a positive way as an explicit part of managing for improvement and quality learning.

Teacher appraisal

Teacher appraisal is still in its infancy and this section is merely a gloss on it (see Bollington, 1990, and Dean, 1991, as useful introductions). The White Paper 'Teaching Quality', published in 1983, was one of the first indications from government that appraisal would eventually be demanded in schools. Pilot studies were established in six LEAs and a Circular was issued in 1988 requiring schools to introduce teacher appraisal within the next four years (McMahon, 1989). It was finally made compulsory in a letter dated 10 December 1990 to Chief Education Officers from the Secretary of State for Education laying down regulations for the appraisal of all teachers and headteachers on a two-year cycle.

The purposes of appraisal need to be made explicit within schools and within departments. The Secretary of State's letter provides a useful starting point for this. I would suggest that history departments need to consider the following features of appraisal:

- Appraisal should help teachers identify ways of enhancing their professional skills and provide help for those teachers having difficulties with their performance. It provides an opportunity for praising what is good and dealing with the unsatisfactory.

- Appraisal should be responsive to the particular needs of individual teachers within history departments.

- Appraisal should be related to establishing in-service needs of teachers and should enable them to recognise their own potential for professional development.

- Appraisal should provide a means of co-ordinating the work of history departments.

- Appraisal should provide heads of history, as appraisers, with information about what is happening in their departments so that they can develop a more accurate view of departmental achievement and shortcomings.

- Appraisal should be continuous and systematic. Because it is structured and cyclical it can regularise review and development.

- Appraisal should be an explicit feature of departmental management not something divorced from it.

Clear purposes need to be accompanied by a clear process. Nationally, appraisal schemes vary but there are certain common principles that underpin them (developed from Suffolk LEA, 1988, quoted in Bollington, 1990, p.9):

- Appraisal must be *objective*. This means that evidence has to be collected that is used as part of the process of evaluating individual teachers.

- It must be *honest* and give an accurate picture of where individual teachers stand.

- It must have *validity*. Without justificatory evidence and example and without an open approach any appraisal process will lack validity in the eyes of those being appraised.

- Results must be achieved through *dialogue* and *agreement*. Appraisal is a two-way street and opportunity for listening and talking by both parties must be an explicit feature of the process.

- It must be *developmental*. Strengths and weakness need to be identified to agree targets for future improvement.

- It must be *effective* and *realistic*. Realisable action plans with mutually agreed targets and dates must be the outcome of individual appraisal.

Effective appraisal as a means of improving teacher performance in history cannot occur in isolation. It should be a logical part of the TQM systems established by departments (see Trethowan, 1991). Where these exist the preconditions for appraisal as a means of action and improvement in quality learning will already be present. There will be a significant consensus about values within departments. There will be an atmosphere of trust, open-mindedness and respect for each other's professionalism and a recognition that all teachers are capable of development and change. The organisational ethos will be a positive one in which the prime imperative will be the development of quality student learning.

So what does this mean in practice for history teachers? The mechanics of the appraisal system will vary between different schools. In essence, however, the four stage model of appraisal developed during the School Teacher Appraisal Study contains its basic components.

Stage 1

There will be an *initial review meeting* between the appraiser and the appraisee at which the limits for appraisal will be established. At the heart of each teacher's appraisal will be the ways in which they develop quality student learning. There is a case for an area for appraisal agreed in advance by teachers within history departments: for example, the ways in which teachers evaluate student learning or how they encourage effective learning in girls. I have found that self-evaluation by the appraisee at this stage is very helpful. It concentrates the reflections of the appraisee and allows this meeting to be more focused. This needs to be linked to the individual's job description. By the end of a meeting, lasting no more than an hour, the following will have been established:

- *Agreed areas for appraisal*. History teachers, however, do not have a single role. They are classroom teachers but also form tutors and managers and they will be teachers in the future. These need to be taken into account when determining the areas to be appraised.

- *When classroom observation will occur and the range of 'other' data to be collected*. A head of history may well have a deputy head or head of year in her department and this role, as well as the departmental role, will need to be considered as well. This may mean interviewing the deputy head of year or the deputy head (pastoral) to obtain information for the dialogue session.

- *A timescale for the whole process*. This is important for both parties. My experience as an appraiser leads me to conclude that the timescale for any appraisal should not normally extend beyond four weeks otherwise valuable momentum will be lost.

Stage 2

This will be followed by the *collection of data*. This consists of classroom observation, the gathering of other evidence and, if not part of stage 1, appraisee self-evaluation. Data gathering needs to be as objective as possible and has two specific functions: it provides information for the appraisal interview and it is a professional development activity in itself. Classroom observation forms a central part of this though appraisers should not view it as the sole source of data. The objective should be to amass as much information about the appraisee as possible since this will help the appraisal process to be as wide-ranging as possible.

Much has been written about classroom observation: for example, Good and Brophy (1987), Wragg (1984). Despite the importance of classroom observation in government thinking Wragg (1994) found that a quarter of his sample were only observed once and that in about a quarter of cases the appraiser actually participated in the lesson. If there is a collaborative approach to teaching and learning within history departments this should not be 'unnatural' and lesson observation should be a normal feature of learning on the job. The focus of the observation will have been agreed in advance, for example, how the teacher deals with the chronology of the English Civil War with a Year 8 class. I have found that a feedback session using a written report specifically on the observation is a valuable thing to do before the dialogue interview. though Wragg (1994) found that this only occurred with a third of his sample.

Stage 3

The *appraisal interview* or 'dialogue' reviews the evidence and establishes an action plan containing targets for the appraisee. An agreed appraisal record is then produced. Trethowan (1991) identifies five key appraisal interview skills:

- *Giving feedback*. The information obtained from data collection needs to be shared with the appraisee. It needs to be specific, descriptive and backed up with clear examples and evidence. The focus should be on what teachers do, not with who or what they are. At this stage the appraiser is non-judgmental.

- *Climate creation* for disclosure from the teacher or allowing the appraisee to 'open up'. Trust and dialogue are crucial between the two people involved.

- *Active listening*. Teachers are not good at listening and tend to view it as a passive rather than active process. The appraiser will inevitably be taking notes and will need, on occasions, to review what has been discussed to make sure that he has understood accurately what has been said and agreed and sometimes not agreed.

- *Asking questions.* The same criteria apply to asking questions in appraisal dialogues as with students. Avoid closed questions. Seek clarification. Give appraisees time to reflect on their answers.

- *Setting targets.* Wragg (1994) found that 90 per cent of appraisals ended with targets for the future, two targets on average, mainly to do with class management and teaching methods.

This process will allow dialogue on the performance of the history teacher and let clear and agreed targets be developed. The outcome of the dialogue will then be written up by the appraiser including the agreed targets and deadlines and a copy given to the appraisee for comment, if any, and signature.

Stage 4

This is followed up by the *target review* – discussions and meetings between appraiser and appraisee to review the achievement of targets as part of overall professional development. On a two year cycle follow-up tends to take place the following year. I would, however, argue strongly that target review needs to take place more regularly to ensure that improvement is being made and to see whether further staff development is necessary.

TQM establishes clear performance indicators that are used to evaluate the effectiveness and quality of change on student learning: for a different approach see Elliott (1989). A collaborative approach to managing history makes this type of appraisal far less threatening since a framework of teacher reflection and self-evaluation is a continuous part of professional development.

The inspector calls

In this section I want to examine briefly where OFSTED can fit into history departments' strategies for improvement in quality learning, rather than consider the mechanics of inspection. See Orston and Shaw (1993) and Brown (1994c), the first for a general perspective, the second specifically for approaches history departments can use. The aim for heads of history is to ensure that the management processes and system for inspection fit as closely as possible with those that departments already have in place for achieving their aims. Confident departments will allocate less time and fewer resources specifically to preparation for inspection. Inspection may be an important driving force for change in history departments but the criterion for any change should not be 'will this look good to the inspectors'. The focus should be whether change helps departments achieve their aims more effectively and efficiently.

A crucial distinction can be made between whether inspection is seen as quality control or as part of the process of assuring quality in teaching and learning. Where quality control is seen as more important inspection takes a central role, but it has a lower profile in quality assurance where it validates what history departments are already doing. This can be seen in the two models in Figure 6.1.

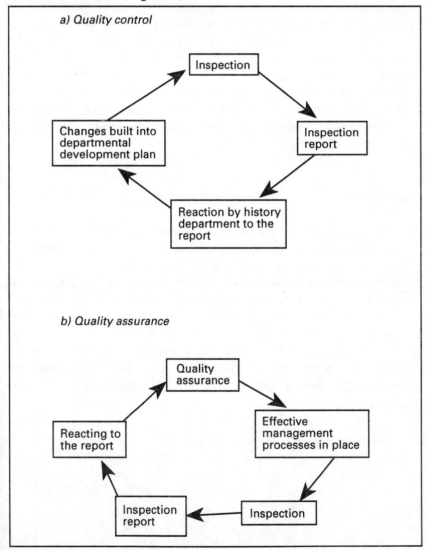

Figure 6.1 Alternative models for OFSTED inspection

128

Where heads of history view inspection in terms of quality control, the object is to find fault and then to apply corrective measures. In this model, departments and teachers can be found wanting and this will result in demoralisation. Departments will step on to a four-yearly treadmill where inspections are the dominant factor in departmental planning. It will result in a reactive environment where teachers and heads of department will spend much of their time reacting to the last report and working to the targets for improvement set by the inspection team. Quality assurance allows departments to handle inspection as part of a process of continuing improvement in their services. Departments already operating with quality assurance and TQM will be better placed to handle changes required as a result of inspection. OFSTED should provide confirmation of the quality of what is being delivered and learned. It should reinforce the directions history departments are developing, the strategies they employ and the ethos they generate. Successful departments are those that provide leadership for staff and for students, deal effectively and successfully with demands for change and improvement and generate quality student learning.

Conclusions

Evaluation, whether it is for students, teachers or history departments, is conducted to bring about improvements in practice. It is an explicit part of the learning, teaching and managing processes. It is essentially formative, concerned with identifying how departments and teachers can do their jobs more effectively and so increase students' ability to learn. It demands that history teachers and history students reflect on what they are doing critically and, as a consequence, develop new, challenging targets that they wish to accomplish. It starts with the collection and analysis of data and ends by facilitating action for improvement and change. It is the logical outcome of collaborative approaches to teaching and learning.

CHAPTER 7

Training Teachers

Plant manager Rucker bubbled about the possibility of continuous improvement processes that marry the two organizations...In the end, he added, 'when something goes wrong, yeah, the organization is leaner and meaner and you can solve problems quicker. But you mainly ought to be thinking about when things are going right. How do you learn, how do you get better?

Peters (1993, pp.404–5)

Students bring a variety of experiences to school and these affect significantly the learning that takes place. Their social context powerfully influences their opportunities to play an active role in their culture and to use what education brings them. It is the job of the history teacher to collaborate with the student and with society in increasing student abilities to learn. The purpose of staff development is to raise the ability of teachers to engage in that collaboration. Staff development has gradually evolved from an *ad hoc* patchwork of courses and workshops into a system ensuring that teachers regularly boost their academic knowledge and professional performance and develop their abilities to learn. Successful history departments must be learning organisations concerned to achieve a high quality product through a process of continuous improvement.

This chapter considers how human resource development can occur in history departments through three issues. Firstly, the nature of learning organisations and the assumptions that underpin them need to be explored. Secondly, the character of staff development and its benefits for student learning are examined. Finally, the question of teacher training is considered. Teaching history is not something that is learned once. It is a continuous process of development, of refinement and reflection. In that sense all teachers remain students throughout their careers.

History departments as learning organisations

Learning processes by history departments can be divided into four critical areas:

1. *We learn with our clients.* Collaborative techniques of teaching and learning require constant learning exchanges with clients. For example, student evaluation, whether formal or informal, allows continuous appraisal of teaching and learning programmes. Taking account of this allows history departments and individual teachers to be responsive and, as a result, to adapt their services to client needs and problems.

2. *We learn from outsiders.* We have to ask how history departments tap the knowledge of consultants, academics, higher education, members of the community and various others. Oral history projects, for example, ask students and teachers to interact with people in their communities.

3. *We learn from each other.* History teachers bring different experiences, expertise and values to the organisation. How is this knowledge passed on within departments? How does it enable departments to become more effective as teams in developing student learning?

4. *We learn within a whole-school environment.* How do history departments fit into overall strategic planning of staff development? Is there a full-blown learning mechanism in place?

Joyce and Showers (1988) base their analysis of staff development on six assumptions. These provide an excellent set of principles that history departments can develop when planning how to become learning organisations:

1. *We should develop comprehensive resource-development systems for education personnel.* The implicit assumption of teacher training in the past was that it provided all the knowledge and skills necessary throughout teachers' careers. The prospect of promotion induced teachers to take additional qualifications like Advanced Diplomas and MA courses. These tended to be provided by experts not necessarily aware of the needs of teachers or schools or of the importance of matching provision to needs and took place away from the 'chalk-face' of the classroom. Individual teachers, generally early in their careers, took responsibility for this and there is ample evidence that many teachers, having reached a certain point on the salary scale, did not engage in any voluntary development for the remainder of their careers. This approach failed, especially as it was generally unsupported by a

broader programme of staff development within institutions. A learning organisation has staff development embedded within the context of the workplace. It is planned and linked to the continuous development of quality student learning.

2. *Student learning can be greatly increased through human development programmes.* The prime objective of staff development is the improvement of student learning. The benefit to the individual history teacher in terms of student motivation and success is a consequence of this.

3. *Staff development should be properly planned.* Recent research on staff development has demonstrated that virtually all teachers can learn the most powerful and complex teaching strategies provided that staff development is properly planned. Poor or irrelevant staff development leads to little overall improvement in the quality of learning. Without strategic planning heads of history will not be able to develop continuous improvement within their departments.

4. *Move out of isolation.* The norms of the workplace of teaching – the school – need to change if powerful staff development is to be implemented; reciprocally, when it is implemented, the energy of the workplace increases considerably. The move away from teachers working in isolated environments towards a collaborative approach to teaching and learning enhances the ability of history departments and teachers to develop continuous improvement in quality learning.

5. *Development should be embedded in professional life.* Embedded staff development will have a great effect on the ethos of the profession and on the beliefs and behaviour of the professional community. History teachers frequently make many of their decisions about teaching and learning on the basis of their own personal knowledge. While not denying the importance of experience, a system of initial training and subsequent staff development will enable them to ground their decision-making on the products of recent research.

6. *We stress that professional knowledge consists of three overlapping components.* These are: the study of academic content; the study of curricular and instructional strategies; and the process of school improvement. Continuous improvement in history is a consequence of knowing what is taught, the most effective ways of teaching it, and the social context in which learning occurs.

Effective staff development increases student learning, increases collaboration within history departments and with students and enables the process of continuous improvement through TQM to irradiate what departments do. It will not lead to history departments becoming learning organisations (Garratt, 1987). This is a result of the processes discussed earlier in the book. However, without it, they cannot become organisations in which learning, at all levels, is an explicit feature of effective management.

Staff development for improvement

Staff development is an essential feature of any organisation that wishes to move forwards towards an agreed vision or to specific objectives (Burke, 1987; Wideen, 1987; Hewton, 1988; O'Sullivan, 1988; Dean, 1991). It provides the vehicle through which history teachers learn what they need to do to be more effective in the classroom and through which they can develop quality student learning. It allows members of history departments to come together to explore new ideas and ways forward as well as to mix socially. Staff development is the essence of a collaborative approach to management.

Defining training needs

Heads of history need sensitivity to balance the individual needs of teachers and the requirements of their departments. It is essential that teacher professional development is not lost in departmental programmes of development for reasons of *esprit de corps* as well as the preservation of some professional status in history teaching. A collaborative approach to managing learning in history can help ensure that a balance is kept. It is also important to distinguish between staff development as *training* and staff development as continuing professional *education*. Training is of value where there is a gap between the knowledge, skills and attitudes necessary for a job and the knowledge, skills and attitudes of history teachers carrying out the job. The introduction of new national initiatives like GCSE, the National Curriculum and teacher appraisal were undertaken very much in the training mode using 'cascade methods'. For most history teachers this was focused on the classroom skills and techniques for dealing with educational principles that had already been decided. The success of training could be determined by whether teachers were able to implement nationally agreed schemes more effectively after training than they would have been had the training not occurred. Professional education is less easy to define. It is personal, individualistic and developmental and can be difficult to quantify. It begins from the premise of what teachers need to perform better. It implies a reflective and collaborative approach to finding solutions to problems. Heads of history will use both approaches in developing the ability of their teachers to ensure quality student learning.

The identification of staff development needs is an important feature of the role of heads of history. This occurs in departments but takes place within the broader framework of whole-school staff development programmes and is invariably linked to the forward planning and budgetary process contained in annual departmental curriculum plans. There must, however, be a significant degree of flexibility so that departments can be adaptive to newly identified needs. Heads of history should keep the following questions in mind when identifying the training needs of their staff (O'Sullivan, 1988, p.11):

● *What are the training needs of history teachers in the department?* An informal process of needs identification will have taken place throughout the year. This should be combined with discussion with staff, linked (but not exclusively) to teacher appraisal, to ensure that heads of departments' perceptions of staff needs are accurate.

● *Are the identified needs particular to individual teachers or general across a department?* This affects the type of training that is developed. Individuals may need to be directed towards particular courses but a whole department need may be better dealt with internally using consultants or the local education authority advisory service.

● *What kind of training is needed to meet each need?*

● *What is the cost of training?* This is increasingly important. Value for money is now the norm as far as training is concerned and heads of history will need to decide priorities within any given year. The cost of training has to be seen in relation to its potential outcome.

● *What will be the benefits of the training and how will this be monitored?* It is important that the outcomes of training are quantifiable. There is little point a teacher going on an external course costing £200 for two days, plus the necessary supply cover, if the consequences of training are not communicated to the rest of a history department or if what has been learned is not translated into the classroom in terms of improved student learning.

The personal training needs of history teachers fall into four main types according to Morant (1981):

1. *Induction.* This applies to the needs of new teachers or experienced teachers in a new post. Training of new heads of department falls into this category.

2. *Extension.* The achievement of additional academic qualifications or job specific study is central to this. This may be seen as promoting the professional development of teachers and has been accorded a lower priority in government thinking than the other three.

3. *Refreshment.* The avoidance of 'staleness', either after some years in the job or when returning to teaching after a career break, is seen as important in developing quality learning in the classroom.

4. *Conversion.* This is needed when teaching a new subject (lateral conversion) or when increasing managerial responsibilities after promotion (vertical conversion).

Each type of need generates its own form of training and heads of history need to be aware of the important differences between them when establishing training priorities within their departments. Developing a new A level course with different teachers responsible for delivery provides a good case for conversion courses while a refresher course may be appropriate for a member of a department who has taught for ten years and has got into something of a rut.

Heads of history, teachers and staff development

The primary role of heads of history is to provide learning opportunities for staff as well as students. This recognises the richness of learning at whatever level. Staff development within departments can occur in a range of situations. It may be:

- *Self-initiated*: an individual teacher may read a book or article that she feels would be of value to others in the department.

- *The result of informal discussions in the staffroom.*

- *Semi-informal:* the department may, for example, have a discussion with a representative from an examining board or an adviser.

- *Formal*: this includes organised INSET subject-specific events like conferences for heads of department or more general whole-school training sessions on quality learning or evaluation.

The effective head of history will promote individual learning opportunities with appropriate levels of support and challenge. Self-initiated staff development is likely to be more effective as a medium for adult learning since the motivation comes from the individual rather than from outside. Schon (1983) suggests that line managers need to provide approaches that minimise constraints on learning, in which personal experiences can be reflected on, talked about, absorbed and tailored to individual needs. This can develop from self-initiated learning and allows reflection on and sharing of practice. Without this, continuous improvement in student learning is difficult.

Heads of history must recognise that successful staff development cannot occur without two things. Firstly, it requires effective evaluation of what is happening in classrooms, about what is successful and what is not and why. This means providing opportunities for teachers to observe their colleagues at work and to discuss what happened with them. This allows the identification of individual and departmental development needs. Secondly, it provides for staff ownership of the INSET that occurs. Within a collaborative management framework this sense of ownership in change will already be necessary and INSET will be seen as a logical extension of the processes of change management. Where it is not, INSET is likely to be seen as something outside individuals and as something imposed on individuals from outside, in the development of which they have had little or no say. No ownership, no change.

The most effective training within history departments occurs under the following circumstances:

- *Training sessions that involve teachers pooling their expertise.* Start from where teachers are and use their classroom experience as something on which to build. A training session on quality learning might begin with the observations teachers have of each other's lessons. This grounds training in practice and leads to a consideration of theoretical questions rather than the other way round. It provides for ownership and the commitment all teachers have to improve their practice.

- *The outcome of this will be sessions where teachers have the opportunity of approaching common problems in need of a solution.* Initial discussions about existing practice will allow teachers to identify common problems. Brainstorming is a valuable way of exploring thinking and collecting ideas at this stage. Members of a history team are asked for all the ideas they can think of about a particular problem. These are all listed on a flip chart or OHP. The list is then considered and possible ideas selected out from the unlikely or, on occasions, bizarre ones. The role of heads of history, as team leaders, is crucial at this point. Brainstorming can become directionless. It is essential that the ideas are drawn together and that aims and objectives are articulated and organised. This will inevitably mean prioritising them through negotiation with team members and developing an action plan for further training.

- *Training works best where teachers are offered tested strategies to tackle these problems*. There is no point in reinventing the wheel. It can be both time-consuming and demotivating for teachers. If a problem has been identified and the team knows how that problem has been dealt with successfully in another department, it may be better to evaluate it and then, if necessary, modify it to the particular circumstances of your department. This may mean visiting other schools and learning from their experiences. As a method of staff development this is under-used but will extend the expertise and experience of teachers, especially if they have been in an institution for some time.

- *Training works bests where teachers are offered examples of existing good practice*. Teachers may well reflect on their own practice but they are suspicious of training that is seen as too theoretical. Training based on good practice allows history teachers to respond positively since they can see its relevance to their own practice.

- *Simulated real school situations under training conditions are effective methods of staff development*. Role-play is a useful method for developing teacher learning in a number of areas. Its function in developing interviewing skills is well documented. However, there are some problems involved in its use. Adults are often unwilling to play parts, though most people overcome this fairly quickly when they get into the task in hand.

- *Training that employs a variety of delivery methods works well*. Adults, like students, respond best where a variety of learning methods are used. Information can be provided in advance for teachers to look at; for example, an article from *Teaching History*. Use can be made of brainstorming, role-play and in-tray exercises. Outside speakers may be used to provide a different perspective and visits can be made to other schools.

Teachers are under increasing pressure from three directions to deliver quality services. All three pressures have the same objective. They want to improve the quality of teaching and learning for students in schools. They differ on how. Political pressures through appraisal, inspection and demands for value for money suggest that this is how you *must* work. The reality of practice in schools with a consequent focus on crisis management can lead to top-down solutions in departments as well as in schools that are grounded in notions of 'this is how we *will* do it'. Professional pressures, suggesting that this is how we *should* work, have been increasingly made management solutions in the past ten years. There is a tension between personal professional development and staff development within a whole-school context in which the former may lose out. The development of a learning culture within history departments through the development of TQM processes and effective staff development based on identified needs, is one way of coping with these diverse pressures. Effective staff development can move history departments forward to an agreed vision or to specific objectives. It combines the two elements necessary for achieving effective student learning in history. Firstly, it recognises the importance of developing people's expertise in teaching and learning. Newton and Tarrant (1992) maintain that:

> We believe that the best investment is in people and improving schools is the improvement of the personal effectiveness of the people, especially the teachers. If teachers feel well regarded, seen as an asset by the school, treated with respect and given access to ways of improving their skills, the school may retain staff for longer than average.

We neglect the human dimension at our peril. Secondly, it recognises that continuous improvement is about identifying needs and developing processes to enable those needs to be met. There is always something new to learn in teaching. New content and research are continually demonstrating that there are new and better ways of enabling students to learn. Teachers need induction, renewal and redirection in the same way as TQM if they are to have the capacity for continuing and career-long development.

Training teachers

Fullan (1993) suggests that society has failed its teachers in two ways. It criticises teachers for not producing better results. At the same time, it does not improve the conditions that would make success possible. A real 'catch 22'. He is rightly critical of teacher educators and teachers for failing to help break the 'catch 22' cycle, maintaining that 'teacher education still has the honour of being simultaneously the worst problem and the best solution in education'.

A tall order!

The last ten years has seen a growing commitment by history departments in schools to initial teacher training (Furlong *et al.*, 1988; Wilkin, 1990,

1992). The language used varies: apprenticeship, internship, partnership, mentoring. The outcome is the same. Student teachers, largely as a result of government prescription, are spending more time in classrooms learning how to teach. Heads of history have seen their role change from supervision of students on their teaching practice to having groups of students working in their departments (often for considerable periods of time), being involved in their overall assessment and playing a far more active role in developing their expertise. It has not, however, been a process without its critics. Rudduck (1992) calls the enterprise 'les liaisons dangereuses'. She suggests that the degree to which such partnerships succeed will depend on several factors:

- Are the partners prepared to give up their traditional views of each other? The old cliché that those who can teach and those who can't teach teachers has a long history. Training institutions and schools must learn to respect each other's strengths and recognise each other's needs and conditions if partnership is to work effectively.

- They must build a shared commitment to agreed principles and purposes. A collaborative process is essential.

- They must recognise that it is a partnership. Pressure from one part of the system may interfere with change in another part. Change will be relatively slow and ways have to be found to maintain momentum.

- Effective training in both institutions is essential. Without this ownership will not exist and without ownership there will be ineffective training.

- Whatever system is developed it cannot interfere with the prime imperative of schools to develop quality learning by students.

These are difficult things to achieve but without them partnership cannot persist and initial teacher training will not be effective.

The changes in teacher education represent a fundamental challenge to the culture of schools, training institutions and teachers and, if they are to be successful, demand the development of schools as learning organisations. The essentials of teacher training have moved away from courses in the history, philosophy and social foundations of education towards a focus on the teacher-as-learner in the classroom. This process should facilitate the development of a career-long continuum of teacher learning where the work of pre-service education, staff development and continuous improvement in schools are viewed as inseparable components of the same work. We are still at an early stage in this process but at present the weakest link in educational reform is the initial preparation and on-job development of teachers.

History departments and initial teacher training

How are history teachers to meet the challenge of preparing tomorrow's history teachers? (Lucas and Watts, 1992) Two research projects on the training of history teachers, based respectively at Leicester and Cambridge Universities, in the late 1980s provide a useful starting-point (Patrick, 1987, 1988, and Booth, Shawyer and Brown, 1988, 1990). They found that the progressive development of students' professional competence was dependent on the extent and effectiveness of the reflection and evaluation of classroom practice undertaken and observed. Reflection and evaluation must deal with both the immediate practicalities of the situation and with learning outcomes and their theoretical underpinning if professional learning is to take place. If this is to occur the research found that there has to be a close relationship between school-based and training institution-based elements of the course. This has been reinforced by subsequent findings (see the paper by Robert Phillips in Lucas and Watts, 1992, and those by David Kerr and Chris Husbands in John and Lucas, 1994).

For there to be successful partnership Booth et al. (1988) call for a broadening of teachers' conception of their role in initial teacher training. This involves '...a partnership directed towards making the whole of a training process a coherent, progressive package.' This view echoes the comments made earlier about schools seeing themselves as learning organisations and teachers as continuous learners. Pendry (1990) suggests that it is important to encourage history teachers in schools to release their own intuitive knowledge of history teaching to student teachers while John (1991) shows how essential professional knowledge or 'teaching-as-professional-craft' can be applied to history teaching. The critical questions history departments and institutions involved in teacher training have to determine are: what are the requirements for teaching to be successful and what are their relationships to quality learning? These questions are at the heart of the successful management of learning history at any level. They provide a means for establishing a career continuum of teacher learning, a unifying theme fundamental to all teaching and learning.

Booth, Shawyer and Brown (1990) use a model of pedagogical reasoning developed initially by Wilson, Shulman and Richert (1987). It is based on three elements:

1. *Comprehension* or what teachers need to know. Teaching requires

knowledge and mastery of five categories:

- Subject content
- The concepts and procedures of the subject
- A range of possible teaching strategies
- The teaching and learning with which students are already familiar
- The knowledge base and existing conceptions of students.

2. *Transformation* or how teachers make subject matter accessible to students. Teaching requires mastery of four categories:

- Matching teaching strategies to objective
- Assessing student learning
- Communication
- Classroom management.

3. *Evaluation and reflection* or how teachers evaluate and reflect on their classroom practice to create new comprehension.

- Evaluation of classroom teaching and learning
- Reflection on that evaluation, leading to new knowledge and understanding and consequently improving practice.

Knowledge is transformed into actions; professional progress and the development of new knowledge can occur only through critical evaluation and reflection of those actions. John (1991) provides a valuable gloss on this model suggesting that the knowledge inherent in the process of history teaching involves:

- Knowledge of the subject matter
- Knowledge of history teaching, which in itself implies:
  - Pedagogical content knowledge: how to teach history
  - Curriculum knowledge: knowing what books and other curriculum material to use
  - Organisational knowledge, including classroom control
- Knowledge of the institution (the school)
- Knowledge of education and the way children learn
- Ideology, which is seen as perhaps the most important, involving:

– Beliefs (philosophy of history)
– Values: what we want to achieve through teaching history
– Attitudes.

These models provide common ground that history departments and training institutions can build on to develop the coherent and practical courses student teachers need if they are to become effective and reflective practitioners in the classroom and capable of developing quality learning by students. It may, as Nigel Proctor optimistically wrote in 1984, 'take very little effort for them to transform the present levels of informal co-operation and collaboration into a lasting partnership beneficial to schools and colleges alike'. The experience of the past ten years suggests that there is still some way to go to achieve this objective.

Mentoring: a way of developing continuous learning

The development of mentoring has been one of the major benefits of the closer partnership between schools and training institutions (Wilkin, 1992; Smith and West-Burnham, 1993). Its principles, originally applied to initial teacher training, do, however, have a broader application to the management of teaching and learning, particularly as a means of developing continuous teacher learning.

Research on history teaching (for example, Burn, 1992; Pendry, 1992, on the Oxford Internship Scheme) provides valuable insights into the concept, processes and problems of mentoring in schools. It is important to be clear what a mentor is. Pendry (1992) suggests that the concept of mentor embedded in the Internship Scheme rests on four key ideas:

1. A mentor is a partner with the training institution method tutor and they are jointly responsible for teacher education.

2. Each partner brings different and distinctive dimensions to the intern's learning but their actions complement each other.

3. The differences in their respective contributions are a result of the nature of the knowledge they have and the positions they hold.

4. The mentor's contribution flows from his/her craft knowledge as a practising school teacher and his/her detailed knowledge and understanding of the particular educational context.

It is the expertise of history teachers in the classroom in developing quality student learning that lies at the heart of this view of mentoring. Student teachers contribute to that learning and play a pivotal role in evaluating that learning. Teachers are no longer simply supervisors ensuring that calm exists in the classroom but provide access to their knowledge in a process of collaborative learning. Mentoring places student learning rather than student control at the forefront of training.

The change from supervisors to mentors will be a long and complex one and we are still in the early stages of making that transition. Is the role of mentor to be one of developing occupational competence or professional confidence and reflection? Is professional craft knowledge to be at the forefront of ITT student development? The role of mentor, as developed from the checklist of the Cheshire LEA, demonstrates some of the tensions that still have to be resolved but also the benefits for career-long professional development of competence-based mentoring schemes (Smith and West-Burnham, 1993, pp.22–3):

- To induct ITT students into the school and department and help to familiarise them with the procedures and practices of both. This induction process is equally applicable to new staff of whatever experience.

- To provide opportunities for informal and formal meetings with appropriate members of staff. This is a case of knowing who to go to with a particular problem or for advice.

- To be responsible for providing professional, social and domestic support.

- To encourage, motivate and create a positive and supportive climate. Successful learning requires this at any level.

- To provide opportunities to observe examples of good practice within school and outside.

- To develop and apply effective procedures of classroom observation. Unstructured observation without any clear focus makes reflection of successful learning difficult.

- To identify particular needs in ITT students and make arrangements for school-based development and support activities.

- To applaud success and celebrate achievement.

- To assist ITT students to recognise and accept their responsibilities with regard to performance, effect and development.

- To use lists of competencies to provide an agenda for focused dialogue and development through targeted action planning.

This process requires a high degree of collaboration in teaching and, would suggest, in teacher learning. Collaborative teaching in history

Burn (1992) suggests, is 'any lesson that is jointly planned and jointly taught by a mentor (or experienced teacher) and a beginning teacher.' Through this, she says, three important kinds of learning can be developed. Firstly, learning to plan lessons carefully involves joint planning with an experienced teacher. This is a valuable process for both. Mentors, particularly if they have been teaching some years and are confident in themselves, often do not make explicit plans. Collaborative teaching makes their plans more explicit. Mentors have to focus on defining the objectives and outcomes of learning and on how differentiated schemes of work are essential for pupils of differing abilities. Secondly, collaborative learning provides ITT students with a protected environment in which to begin developing classroom teaching skills. This enables students to move more quickly from concerns about control to questions about student learning. Throwing students into the deep end is no longer an option. Finally, students can gain access to teachers' craft knowledge and their experience. This is invaluable if students are to become competent classroom teachers rather than effective control agents. A collaborative approach allows for the development of a clear focus on student learning and how it can best be encouraged. By developing different techniques of teaching and flexible approaches to planning, students can move with increasing confidence beyond an emphasis on control towards different methods of teaching history for effective learning.

The skills that teachers develop as mentors have applications far beyond the confines of teacher training. Firstly, they focus on what happens in the classroom and recognise the centrality of that experience to managing learning. Quality learning means taking risks. Student teachers are encouraged to explore their practice and develop untried ways of harnessing learning in their classrooms. This separates learning from control. While successful learning needs a controlled classroom, a controlled classroom does not necessarily result in successful learning. Secondly, they reinforce the argument for collaborative cultures amongst teachers. Thirdly, they demonstrate the diverse nature of good practice in teaching and the possibility of achieving similar goals through a variety of means. Fourthly, they are grounded in reflection on action, in a critique of practice based on classroom observation and experience. Finally, they integrate knowledge about how students learn in the classroom and the processes involved in developing the ability of teachers to teach effectively. Mentoring provides a process, based on the development of the classroom experiences of teachers and students, that furnishes a model for the continuous development of history teachers from initial training and throughout their careers.

CHAPTER 8

Achieving and Maintaining Quality

A manager who attended a seminar I was conducting...supplies me with the metaphor that in various ways runs all through this book. It is the metaphor of 'permanent white water'. 'Most managers are taught to think of themselves as paddling their canoes on calm, still lakes', he said. 'They're led to believe that they should be pretty much able to go where they want, when they want, using means that are under their control...But it's been my experience,' he concluded, 'that you never get out of the rapids!'

Vaill (1989, p.2)

Talk to heads of history and it won't be very long before they'll start telling you how much harder they're working. 'It's all those new initiatives', they say. 'A National Curriculum that is continually changing, teacher appraisal, development plans, a relentless, non-stop pursuit of more and more knowledge about the job and that's before you get into the classroom and start teaching. The present has become turbulent and threatening, chaos is round the corner.' They are, of course, right. What we have to do, as heads of history and as history teachers, is to try and understand the actual world of permanent white water and develop it so that we can achieve quality learning in our students.

To do this we have to recognise that running a history department or simply teaching history is not the same as it was ten years ago and that it never can be the same. We have to forget the past and look to the future. This is challenging because the future is uncertain, threatening and unpredictable. We need to revise certain principles about management as they can prevent us moving forward. Firstly, we have to challenge the myth that a single person manages history departments. This assumes that there is a coherent role to be performed. The reality in many departments is that every teacher plays a critical role in managing student learning. The head of department may provide direction or vision but unless this is shared effective management of learning and continuous improvement of learning will prove difficult. Secondly, hierarchy – the notion of having someone to report to – is another myth that is deeply ingrained in our psyche: having someone in charge means that departments are properly organised. Control from the top works but it strangles creativity and initiative, dulls teachers' sensitivities and cramps their style. Anyway, the genie is out of the bottle, management by 'tablets of stone' is redundant, as successive Secretaries of State have discovered. Thirdly, we are reaching the limits of the model that says that effective action is a process of rationally working out what needs to be done and then rationally doing it. The notion of outrageous goals, of working with unpredictability, of intuition and feeling and the value they bring in understanding and developing student learning, suggest that our impulse to crush a problem with rational analysis may not be serving us so effectively as we believe. This situation has produced what has been called 'the Grand Paradox of Management'. To be a manager today is to take responsibility for controlling what is less and less controllable. As the world becomes less stable and predictable, the paradox intensifies.

Old management principles don't die by themselves. They die when more apt principles are developed – principles that fit better with people's experiences, that take account more fully of what is going on around us and that help explain the unpredictable. The development of goals has been an accepted part of managing history departments for some years. We are, however, seeing more and more emphasis on accountability and results as, at the same time, achieving them becomes more uncertain. It is no longer possible to manage existing systems. The instability of the organisational environment threatens to make any given structure and set of policies out of balance with the demands and opportunities made of them. The precedence of leadership over simply managing has never been more imperative. Leaders within history departments constantly develop strategies and processes consciously to improve the ability of the system to adapt to its present and future environments. This means the need to go forward with a heightened awareness of what the risks are.

Leadership is, however, shared within the team. Much has been written on effective teamwork but it remains a fragile idea. Just when it is needed most, it seems hardest to practice. There are many disincentives. Reward systems focus on individual rather than team achievement, a reflection of the individualistic bias of our culture. Yet all other styles of management obviously detract from getting the work done in the increasingly interdependent environment of schools. Teamwork does not happen by accident or automatically and certainly is not the result of the energies of a single leader. Team members have to talk to each other and this calls for a collaborative culture of collective self-awareness, openness and maturity.

Managing history in schools today is about empowering people whether they are teachers or students. When we are trying to understand why students do or do not learn history successfully, we are concerned with providing them with the power to understand and develop. Quality learning for one student might be at lower level than for another. We judge this, however, not by whether students have achieved at this level or that but whether the process of learning has empowered them to learn further, to improve continuously the quality of what they are doing. The same applies to teachers. Quality teaching is concerned with empowering teachers to improve the quality of their teaching in relation to the learning achievements of their students. The medium of Total Quality Management, by focusing management on what occurs in the learning process, empowers departments towards the process of continuous improvement. It recognises the unpredictability and riskiness of change and builds this into a holistic vision of where teachers, students and history departments can steer in the permanent white waters in which they find themselves. Cliché though it undoubtedly is, no one solution is right. There are no blueprints for developing change or for continuous improvement or for achieving quality. There is only collaboration by people.

References

Adair, J. (1987) *Effective Teambuilding*. London: Pan.

Adelman, C. (ed.) (1984) *The Politics and Ethics of Evaluation*. London: Croom Helm.

Aspinwall, K., Simkins, T., Wilkinson, J.F. and McAuley, M.J. (1992) *Managing Evaluation in Education*. London: Routledge.

Atkinson, R.F. (1978) *Knowledge and Explanation in History*. London: Macmillan.

Ballard, M. (ed.) (1970) *New movements in the study and teaching of history*. London: Temple Smith.

Barker, R. (1981) History Abandoned, *Teaching History*, **30**, pp.13–14.

Becher, T. and Maclure, S. (1987) *Accountability in Education*. Windsor: NFER.

Bell, L. (1992) *Managing Teams in Secondary Schools*. London: Routledge.

Ben Jones, R. (ed.) (1973) *Practical Approaches to the New History*. London: Hutchinson.

Bennis, W. and Nanus, B. (1985) *Leaders*. New York: Harper & Row.

Blake, C. (1959) Can History be Objective?, in Gardiner, P. (ed.) *Theories of History*, pp.329–343. London: Macmillan.

Bollington, R., Hopkins, D. and West, M. (1990) *An Introduction to Teacher Appraisal*. London: Cassell.

Booth, M. (1969) *History Betrayed*. Harlow: Longman.

Booth, M., Shawyer, G. and Brown, R. (1988) Survival or Training?, *Teaching History*, **50**, pp.16–19.

Booth, M., Shawyer, G. and Brown, R. (1990) Partnership and the training of student history teachers, in Booth, M., Furlong, J. and Wilkin, M. (eds) *Partnership in Initial Teacher Training*, pp.99–109. London: Cassell.

Borich, G.D. and Jemelka, R.P. (1982) *Programs and Systems: An Evaluation Perspective*. New York: Academic Press.

Boswell, T. (1994) Speech to The Future of A levels, NEAB Conference, 9 May.

Bourdillon, H. (1988) Lessons in history – beyond the male-stream classroom, in Chester, G. and Nielsen, S. (eds) *In Other Words – Writing as a Feminist*. London: Hutchinson.

Bourdillon, H. (1994) H. Bourdillon On the record: the importance of gender in teaching history, in Bourdillon, H. (ed.) *Teaching History*, pp.62–75. London: Routledge.

Brown, R. (1991a) *Pupil Behaviour and School Effectiveness*, mimeo.

Brown, R. (1991b) *Squaring the circle or a curriculum for the twenty-first century*, mimeo.

Brown, R. (1992a) *The Curriculum and the Market or Marketing the Curriculum?*, mimeo.

Brown, R. (1992b) *Phasing Change: a potent scenario*, mimeo.

Brown, R. (1992c) *Strategies for Change: a policy on gender*, mimeo.

Brown, R (1993) *Student expectations of history at transfer: a subjective analysis of five cohorts*, mimeo

Brown, R (1994a) History and post-16 vocational courses, in Bourdillon, H. (ed.) *Teaching History*, pp.91-97. London: Routledge.

Brown, R. (1994b) Gender Issues, in *Manshead School Humanities Handbook*, mimeo.

Brown, R. (1994c) *Preparing for Inspection in Secondary History: A Practical Guide*. London: The Historical Association.

Brown, S. and McIntyre, D. (1993) *Making Sense of Teaching*. Milton Keynes: Open University Press.

Buchmann, M. (1993) Rule over Person: Morality and Authenticity in Teaching, in Buchmann, M. and Floden, R.E. (eds) *Detachment and Concern: Conversations in the Philosophy of Teaching and Teacher Education*, pp.145–157. London: Cassell.

Burke, P.J. (1987) *Teacher Development: Induction, Renewal and Redirection*. Brighton: Falmer Press.

Burn, C. (1992) Collaborative teaching, in Wilkin, M. (ed.) (1992) *Mentoring in Schools*, pp.133–143. London: Kogan Page.

Bush, T. (ed.) (1980) *Approaches to School Management*. London: Paul Chapman.

Calderhead, J. (ed) (1988) *Teachers' Professional Learning*. Brighton: Falmer Press.

Calderhead, J. (1994) The Reform of Initial Teacher Education and Research on Learning to Teach: Contrasting Ideas, in John, P. and Lucas, P. (eds) *Partnership and Progress: New Developments in History Teacher Education and History Teaching*, pp.59–77. University of Sheffield.

Cangelosi, J.S. (1991) *Evaluating Classroom Instruction*. Harlow: Longman.

Carr, E.H. (1962) *What is History?* London: Penguin.

Clare, J. (1989) Forty Questions to Review your History Department, *Teaching History*, **57**, pp.34–37.

Coltham, J.B. and Fines, J. (1971) *Educational Objectives for the Study of History: a suggested framework.* London: The Historical Association.

Cooper, H. (1992) *The Teaching of History.* London: David Fulton.

Davies, B. and Ellison, L. (1992) *School Development Planning.* Harlow: Longman.

Davies, B. and Pritchard, P. (1975) History Still in Danger, *Teaching History*, **14**, pp.113-115.

Day, C., Calderhead, J. and Denicolo, P. (eds) (1993) *Research on Teacher Thinking: Understanding Professional Development.* Brighton: Falmer Press.

Day, C., Pope, M. and Denicolo, P. (eds) (1990) *Insight into Teachers' Thinking and Practice.* Brighton: Falmer Press.

Dean, J. (1991) *Professional Development in Schools.* Milton Keynes: Open University Press.

Deming, W.E. (1988) *Out of Crisis.* Cambridge: Cambridge University Press.

DES (1988a) *Key Role, Humanities in Society*, 207/88, 7 July. London: DES.

DES (1988b) *The Management of Educational Resources: Effective Secondary Schools.* London: HMSO.

Dickinson, A.K. and Lee, P.J. (eds) (1978) *History Teaching and Historical Understanding.* London: Heinemann.

Dickinson, A.K. and Lee, P.J. (1984) Making sense of history, in Dickinson, A.K., Lee, P.J. and Rogers, P.J. (eds) (1984) *Learning History,* pp.117-153. London: Heinemann.

Dickinson, A.K. and Lee, P.J. (1994) Investigating Progression in Children's Ideas about History: The CHATA Project, in John, P. and Lucas, P. (eds) *Partnership and Progress: New Developments in History Teacher Education and History Teaching,* pp.78–101. Sheffield: University of Sheffield.

Dickinson, A.K., Lee, P.J. and Rogers, P.J. (eds) (1984) *Learning History.* London: Heinemann.

Downey, M.T. and Levstik, L.S. (1991) Teaching and Learning History, in Shaver, J.P. (ed) *Handbook of Research on Social Studies Teaching and Learning,* pp.400–410. New York: Macmillan.

Doyle, W. (1986) Classroom organization and management, in Wittrock, M.C. (ed) *Handbook of Research on Teaching,* third edn. New York: Macmillan.

Drucker, P. (1968) *The Practice of Management*. London: Pan.

Earley, P. and Fletcher-Campbell, F. (1989) *The Time to Manage? Department and faculty heads at work*. Windsor: NFER–Nelson.

Edwards, A. D. (1978) The language of history and the communication of historical knowledge, in Dickinson, A.K. and Lee, P.J.(eds) (1978) *History Teaching and Historical Understanding*, pp.54–71. London: Heinemann.

Elliott, J. (1989) Appraisal of performance or appraisal of persons, in Simon, H. and Elliott. J. (eds) *Rethinking Assessment and Appraisal*, pp.80–99. Milton Keynes: Open University Press.

Eraut, M. (1984) Institution-based curriculum evaluation, in Skilbeck, M., Everard, B. and Morris, G. (eds) *Effective School Management*. London: Paul Chapman.

Eraut, M. (1988) Management Knowledge: its nature and its development, in Calderhead, J. (ed.) *Teachers' Professional Learning*, pp.196–204. Brighton: Falmer Press.

Floden, R.E. and Buchmann, M. (1993) Between Routines and Anarchy: preparing teachers for uncertainty, in Buchmann, M. and Floden, R.E. (eds) *Detachment and Concern: Conversations in the Philosophy of Teaching and Teacher Education*, pp.211–221. London: Cassell.

Fullan, M. (1991) *The New Meaning of Educational Change*. London: Cassell.

Fullan, M. (1993) *Change Forces: Probing the Depths of Educational Reform*. Brighton: Falmer Press.

Furlong, V J.P., Hirst, P., Pocklington, K. and Miles, S. (1988) *Initial Teacher Training and the Role of the School*. Milton Keynes: Open University Press.

Garratt, B. (1987) *The Learning Organization and the need for directors who think*. London: Fontana Collins.

Goddard, D. and Leask, M. (1992) *The Search for Quality: Planning for Improvement and Managing Change*. London: Paul Chapman.

Good, T.L. and Brophy, J.E. (1987) *Looking in Classrooms*, fourth edn. New York: Harper & Row.

Goodlad, J., Soder, R. and Sirotnik, K.A. (eds) (1990) *The Moral Dimensions of Teaching*. San Francisco: Jossey-Bass.

Hallam, R.N. (1970) Piaget and thinking in history, in Ballard, M. (ed.) *New Movements in the Study and Teaching of History*, pp.162–178. London: Temple Smith.

Hallam, R.N. (1972) Thinking and learning in history, *Teaching History*, **2**, p.337.

Hargreaves, A. (1994) *Changing Teachers, Changing Times: Teachers' work and culture in the post-modern age*. London: Cassell.

Harper, P. (1993) Using the Attainment Targets in Key Stage 2: AT2, Interpretations of History, *Teaching History*, **72**, pp.11–13.

Harvey-Jones, J. (1988) *Making It Happen: Reflections on Leadership*. London: Collins.

Haslam, J. (1986) Why Integrate?, in Holly, D. (ed.) *Humanities in Adversity*, pp.9–21. Brighton: Falmer Press.

Hastings, C., Bixby, P. and Chaudhry-Lawton, R. (1986) *Superteams: A Blueprint for Organisational Success*. London: Fontana.

Healy, T. (1994) New Historicism, *English Review*, **23**, p.13.

Hewton, E. (1988) *School Focused Staff Development: Guidelines for Policy Makers*. Brighton: Falmer Press.

Higham, J. (1979) How to Evaluate a History Department, *Teaching History*, **24**, pp.14–17.

Hodkinson, A. (1995) Historical time and the National Curriculum, *Teaching History*, **79**.

Hopkins, D. (1989) *Evaluation for School Development*. Milton Keynes: Open University Press.

Jackson, P.W. (1986) *The practice of teaching*. New York: Teachers College Press.

Jahoda, G. (1962) Children's concepts of time and history, *Educational Review*, **95**.

James, M. (1989) Negotiation and dialogue in student assessment and teacher appraisal, in Simon, H. and Elliott, J. *Rethinking Appraisal and Assessment*, pp.149–160. Milton Keynes: Open University Press.

Jenkins, K. (1991) *Re-thinking History*. London: Routledge.

Jenkins, K. (1995) *What is History? From Carr and Elton to Rorty and White*. London: Routledge.

Jenkins, K. and Brickley, P. (1986) A Level History: From Skillology to Methodology, *Teaching History*, **46**, pp.3–7.

John, P. (1991) The professional craft knowledge of the history teacher, *Teaching History*, **64**, pp.8–12.

John, P. and Lucas, P. (eds) (1994) *Partnership and Progress: New Developments in History Teacher Education and History Teaching*. Sheffield: University of Sheffield.

Joyce, B. and Showers, B. (1988) *Student Achievement through Staff Development*. New York: Longman.

Keelan, P. and Dickinson, A.K. (1991) History and the Humanities, in Gordon, P. (ed.) *Teaching the Humanities*, pp.88–107. London: Woburn Press.

Klein, G. (1993) *Education Towards Race Equality*. London: Cassell.

Kyriacou, C. (1986) *Effective Teaching in Schools*. Oxford: Basil Blackwell.

152

Kyriacou, C. (1991) *Essential Teaching Skills*. Oxford: Basil Blackwell.

Lally, J. and West, J. (1981) *The Child's Awareness of the Past – Teacher's Guide*. Hereford & Worcester County History Advisory Committee.

Leff, G. (1969) *History and Social Theory*. London: Merlin.

Licht, B. and Dwerck, C. (1987) Sex differences in achievement orientations, in Arnot, M. and Weiner, G. (eds) *Gender and the Politics of Schooling*. Milton Keynes: Open University Press.

Limm, P. R. (1980) History: the search for a balanced rationale, *Teaching History*, **28**, pp.25–28.

Louis, K. and Miles, M. B. (1990) *Improving the Urban High School: What Works and Why*. Brighton: Falmer Press.

Lucas, P. and Watts, R. (eds) (1992) *Meeting the Challenge: Preparing Tomorrow's History Teachers*. Sheffield: Standing Conference of History Teacher Educators in the United Kingdom, in association with the University of Sheffield Division of Education.

McMahon, A. (1989) *School Teacher Appraisal Schemes in England: The Pilot Scheme Experience*, in Wilson, J.D., Thomson, G.O.B., Millward, R.E. and Keenan T. (eds) *Assessment for Teacher Development*, pp.175–182. Brighton: Falmer Press.

Majaro, S. (1988) *The Creative Gap: Managing Ideas for Profit*. Harlow: Longman.

Marland, M. (1971) *Head of Department: Leading a Department in a Comprehensive School*. London: Heinemann.

Marland, M. (1975) *The Craft of the Classroom: A Survival Guide*. London: Heinemann.

McAleavy, T. (1993) Using the Attainment Targets in Key Stage 3: AT2, Interpretations of History, *Teaching History*, **72**, pp.14–17.

McGovern, C. (1994) This history curriculum is bunk, *The Times*, May 7, p.16.

Montesquieu, Charles-Louis de Secondat, Baron de (1748) *De L'Esprit des Lois*. Paris: Gallimard, 1970 edn.

Morant, R.W. (1981) *In-Service Education within the School*. London: Allen and Unwin.

Morgan, C. and Murgatroyd, S. (1994) *Total Quality Management in the Public Sector*. Milton Keynes: Open University Press.

Murgatroyd, S. and Morgan, C. (1993) *Total Quality Management and the School*. Milton Keynes: Open University Press.

Newton, C. and Tarrant, T. (1992) *Managing Change in Schools: a practical handbook*. London: Routledge.

Noddings, N. (1984) *Caring: a feminine approach to ethics and moral education*. Berkeley: University of California Press.

Oakland, J. (1986) *Statistical Process Control*. London: Heinemann.

153

Oakland, J. (1989) *Total Quality Management*. Oxford: Butterworth.

Orston, M. and Shaw, M. (1993) *Inspection: A Preparation Guide for Schools*. Harlow: Longman.

O'Sullivan, F., Jones, K. and Reid, K. (1988) *Staff Development in Secondary Schools*. London: Hodder & Stoughton.

Palmer, M. (1976) Educational Objectives and Source Materials: Some Practical Suggestions, *Teaching History*, **16**, pp.26–30.

Pankhania, J. (1994) *Liberating the National History Curriculum*. Brighton: Falmer Press.

Pascale, P. (1990) *Managing on the Edge*. New York: Touchstone.

Patrick, H. (1987) *The aims of teaching history in secondary schools*, (Occasional Paper). Leicester: School of Education, University of Leicester.

Patrick, H. (1988) History teachers for the 1990s and beyond, *Teaching History*, **50**, pp.10–16.

Patten, J. (1994) Extract from a speech by John Patten, Secretary of State for Education, in Andover on Friday 18 March, *Department for Education News*, 70/94.

Peel, E.A. (1967) Some problems in psychology of history teaching, in Burston, W.H. and Thompson, D. (eds) *Studies in the Nature and Teaching of History*. London: Routledge.

Pendry, A. (1990) Dilemmas for history teacher educators, *British Journal of Educational Studies*, **38**(1), pp.47–62.

Pendry, A. (1992) Mentoring in teacher education, in Lucas, P. and Watts, R. (eds) *Meeting the Challenge: Preparing Tomorrow's History Teachers*, pp.24–36. Sheffield: Standing Conference of History Teacher Educators in the United Kingdom, in association with the University of Sheffield Division of Education.

Peters, T. (1987) *Thriving on Chaos: Handbook for a Management Revolution*. London: Pan.

Peters, T. (1993) *Liberation Management: Necessary Disorganization for the Nanosecond Nineties*. London: Pan.

Peters, T. and Austin, N. (1994 edn) *A Passion for Excellence: The Leadership Difference*. First published 1984. London: Fontana.

Plant, R. (1987) *Managing Change and Making it Stick*. London: Fontana.

Plumb, J.H. (1964) *Crisis in the Humanities*. London: Penguin.

Price, M. (1968) History in Danger, *History*, **53**, pp.342–47.

Pring, R. (1994) Bridging the Academic/Vocational Divide, paper given at *The Future of A levels*, NEAB Conference, 9 May.

Proctor, N. (1984) Towards a partnership with schools, *Journal of Education for Teaching*, **10**(3), pp.219–32.

Ranson, S. (1993) Public education and local democracy, in Tomlinson, H. (ed) *Education and Training 14–19: Continuity and Diversity in the Curriculum,* pp.1–9. Harlow: Longman.

Rogers, P.J. (1979) *The New History: theory into practice.* London: The Historical Association.

Rogers, P.J. (1984) Why Teach History?, in Dickinson, A.K., Lee, P.J. and Rogers, P.J. (eds) *Learning History,* pp.20–38. London: Heinemann.

Rosenholtz, S. (1989) *Teachers' Workplace: The Social Organization of Schools.* New York: Longman.

Rudduck, J. (1988) The Ownership of Change as a Basis for Teachers' Professional Learning, in Calderhead, J. (ed.) (*op. cit.*) pp.205–222.

Rudduck, J. (1992) Universities in partnership with schools and school systems: Les liaisons dangereuses, in Fullan, M. and Hargreaves, A. (eds) *Teacher Development and Educational Change,* pp.194–212. Brighton: Falmer Press.

Rutter *et al.* (1979) *Fifteen Thousand Hours.* Wells: Open Books.

Schaffer, R. (1991) Demand better results and get them. *Harvard Business Review.* **69**(2), pp.142–9.

Schon, D.A. (1983) *The Reflective Practitioner.* London: Temple Smith.

Schon, D.A. (1987) *Educating the Reflective Practitioner.* New Jersey: Jossey-Bass.

Scott, B. (1994) A Post-Dearing Look at Hi2: Interpretations of History, *Teaching History,* **75**, pp.20–26.

Senge, P.M. (1990) *The Fifth Discipline: The Art and Practice of The Learning Organization.* New York: Doubleday.

Shawyer, G., Booth, M. and Brown, R. (1988) The Development of Children's Historical Thinking, *Cambridge Journal of Education,* **18**(2), pp.209–219.

Shemilt, D. (1979) *Schools Council 13-16: Past, Present and Future,* mimeo.

Shemilt, D. (1980) *13-16 Evaluation Study.* Edinburgh: Holmes McDougall.

Shemilt, D. (1986) A babble of voices: adolescent ideas about evidence, in Portal, C. (ed.) *The History Curriculum for Teachers,* pp.39–61. Brighton: Falmer Press.

Shulman, L.S. (1986) Those who understand: knowledge growth in teaching, *Educational Researcher,* **15**, pp.4–14.

Simchowitz, Cheryl-Ann (1995) The Development of Temporal Concepts in children and its significance for history teachers in the senior primary school, *Teaching History,* **79**.

Smith, P. and West-Burnham, J. (eds) (1993) *Mentoring in the Effective School.* Harlow: Longman.

Stake, R. E. (1989) The evaluation of teaching, in Simon, H. and Elliott, J. *Rethinking Appraisal and Assessment*, pp.13-19. Milton Keynes: Open University Press.

Stanford, M. (1994) *A Companion to the Study of History*. Oxford: Basil Blackwell.

Suffolk LEA (1988) *Teacher Appraisal: A Practical Guide*. Ipswich: Suffolk County Council.

Sylvester, D. (1994) Change and continuity in history teaching 1900–93, in Bourdillon, H. (ed.) *Teaching History*, pp.9–26. London: Routledge.

Tansley, P. (1989) *Course Teams: The Way Forward in FE?* Windsor: NFER–Nelson.

The Times Educational Supplement (1984) *1066 and all that...*, 17 February.

Thomas, E. and Woods, M. (1994) *The Manager's Casebook*. London: Penguin.

Thompson, D. (1984) Understanding the past: procedures and content, in Dickinson, A.K., Lee, P.J. and Rogers, P.J. (eds) *Learning History*, pp.168–186. London: Heinemann.

Torrington, D. and Weightman, J. (1989) *The Reality of School Management*. Oxford: Basil Blackwell.

Trethowan, D.M. (1991) *Managing with Appraisal: Achieving Quality Schools through Performance Management*. London: Paul Chapman.

Truckman, B.W. and Jensen, M.A.C. (1977) Stages of small group development revisited, *Groups and Organizational Studies*, **2**, pp.419–42.

Vaill, P.B. (1989) *Managing as a Performing Art: New Ideas for a World of Chaotic Change*. San Francisco: Jossey-Bass.

Wake, R. (1970) History as a Separate Discipline: the case, *Teaching History*, **3**, pp.169–171.

West-Burnham, J. (1992) *Managing Quality in Schools*. Harlow: Longman.

Whitaker, P. (1993) *Managing Change in Schools*. Milton Keynes: Open University Press.

Wideen, M.F. and Andrews, I. (eds) (1987) *Staff Development for School Improvement: A Focus on the Teacher*. Brighton: Falmer Press.

Wilkin, M. (1990) The Development of Partnership in the United Kingdom, in Booth, M., Furlong, J. and Wilkin, M. (eds) *Partnership in Initial Teacher Training*, pp.3–23. London: Cassell.

Wilkin, M. (ed.) (1992) *Mentoring in Schools*. London: Kogan Page.

Wilson, S.M., Shulman, L.S. and Richert, A.E. (1987) 150 different ways of knowing: representations of knowledge in teaching, in Calderhead, J. (ed) *Exploring teachers' thinking*, pp.104–124. London: Cassell.

Woff, R. (1991) The Scope of the Humanities, in Gordon, P. (ed.) *Teaching the Humanities*, pp.12–35. London: Woburn Press.

Wood, S. (1995) Developing an understanding of time – sequencing issues, *Teaching History*, **79**.

Wragg, E.C. (ed.) (1984) *Classroom Teaching Skills*. London: Croom Helm.

Wragg, E.C. (1994) Under the microscope, *The Times Educational Supplement*, 9 September.

Wragg, E.C., Wikeley, F., Wragg, C. and Haynes, G. (1995) *Teacher Appraisal Observed*. London: Routledge.

Index